W9-AFR-177

SENSATIONAL SPORTS TEAMS

Burning Up the Court
THE MIAMI HEAT

Jeff C. Young

 MyReportLinks.com Books
an imprint of
 Enslow Publishers, Inc. E

Box 398, 40 Industrial Road
Berkeley Heights, NJ 07922
USA

To Steve Blackwell (1948–2006)
for encouraging me to pursue my writing

MyReportLinks.com Books, an imprint of Enslow Publishers, Inc. MyReportLinks®
is a registered trademark of Enslow Publishers, Inc.

Library of Congress Cataloging-in-Publication Data

Young, Jeff C., 1948–
  Burning up the court—the Miami Heat / Jeff C. Young.
     p. cm. — (Sensational sports teams)
  Includes bibliographical references and index.
  ISBN-13: 978-1-59845-049-1
  ISBN-10: 1-59845-049-2
  1. Miami Heat (Basketball team)—Juvenile literature. I. Title.
GV885.52.M53Y68 2008
796.323'6409759381—dc22

                                        2006024222

Printed in the United States of America

10 9 8 7 6 5 4 3 2 1

To Our Readers:
Through the purchase of this book, you and your library gain access to the Report Links that specifically back up this book.
The Publisher will provide access to the Report Links that back up this book and will keep these Report Links up to date on **www.myreportlinks.com** for five years from the book's first publication date.
We have done our best to make sure all Internet addresses in this book were active and appropriate when we went to press. However, the author and the Publisher have no control over, and assume no liability for, the material available on those Internet sites or on other Web sites they may link to.
The usage of the MyReportLinks.com Books Web site is subject to the terms and conditions stated on the Usage Policy Statement on **www.myreportlinks.com.**
A password may be required to access the Report Links that back up this book. The password is found on the bottom of page 4 of this book.
Any comments or suggestions can be sent by e-mail to comments@myreportlinks.com or to the address on the back cover.

Photo Credits: AP/Wide World Photos, pp. 1, 3, 6, 12, 14–15, 19, 23, 28, 38, 45, 49, 54–55, 62–63, 71, 76, 78–79, 88, 92–93, 98, 102, 104–105, 107, 110; Basketball-Reference.com, p. 33; CNN/Sports Illustrated, pp. 21, 42, 57; CTV, Inc., p. 53; Dwyane Wade, p. 17; ESPN Internet Ventures, pp. 11, 91, 112; Hoopsworld.com, a Service of Basketball News Services, LLC, p. 96; Hospitality Internet Media, LLC, p. 31; IGN Entertainment, Inc., p. 74; Miami Herald Media Co., p. 114; MSNBC.com, p. 25; Naismith Memorial Basketball Hall of Fame, Inc., p. 46; NBA Media Ventures, LLC, pp. 35, 36, 60, 69, 73, 83; NBRPA, pp. 81, 84, 108; Shutterstock.com, p. 5; SportsLine.com, Inc., pp. 51, 67; Sun-Sentinel Co. & South Florida Interactive, pp. 9, 40; *The Hoya*, p. 64; Washington Post Company, p. 86.

Cover Photo: AP/Wide World Photos

Cover Description: Dwyane Wade burns up the court.

CONTENTS

MyReportLinks.com Books
Great Books, Great Links, Great for Research!

The Internet sites featured in this book can save you hours of research time. These Internet sites—we call them **"Report Links"**—are constantly changing, but we keep them up to date on our Web site.

When you see this "Approved Web Site" logo, you will know that we are directing you to a great Internet site that will help you with your research.

Give it a try! Type http://www.myreportlinks.com into your browser, click on the series title and enter the password, then click on the book title, and scroll down to the Report Links listed for this book.

The Report Links will bring you to great source documents, photographs, and illustrations. MyReportLinks.com Books save you time, feature Report Links that are kept up to date, and make report writing easier than ever! A complete listing of the Report Links can be found on pages 116–117 at the back of the book.

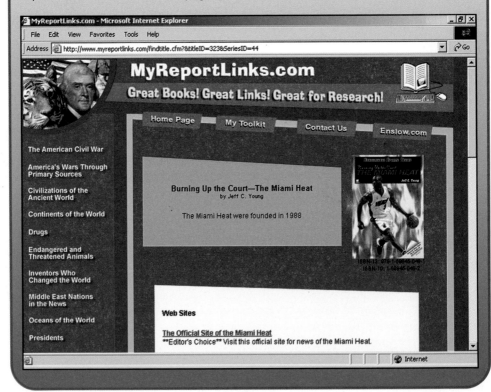

Please see "To Our Readers" on the copyright page for important information about this book, the MyReportLinks.com Web site, and the Report Links that back up this book.

Please enter **MHB1847** if asked for a password.

MIAMI HEAT TIME LINE

1986—*May 6:* Billy Cunningham and Zev Bufman announce plans to bring an NBA team to Miami.

—*October 16:* Miami Heat is chosen as the name for the new franchise from among twenty thousand entries in a "name-the-team" promotion.

—*December 24:* The Heat reach the NBA's mandated goal of selling ten thousand season tickets.

1988—*June 28:* Miami makes Syracuse University center Rony Seikaly its first pick in the NBA draft (ninth overall).

—*July 11:* Ron Rothstein is hired to be the Heat's first head coach.

—*November 5:* The Heat open their first season by hosting the Los Angeles Clippers before a sellout crowd of 15,008 at the Miami Arena. The Clippers win 101–80.

—*December 14:* The Heat get their first regular season win by defeating the Clippers at Los Angeles, 89–88.

1989—*May 4:* Heat gets its first postseason honor when guard Kevin Edwards is named to the NBA's All-Rookie Second Team.

1992—The Heat make playoffs for first time but are swept by Chicago Bulls, 3–0.

1994—The Heat have their first winning season (42–40), but fall to Atlanta, 3–2, in the first round of the playoffs.

1995—*September 2:* Pat Riley becomes the Heat's president and head coach.

1996—*January 30:* Alonzo Mourning becomes the first Miami Heat player selected to play in the NBA All-Star Game.

1997—*April 10:* Heat clinch their first Atlantic Division title with a 93–83 win over the Pistons.

—*May 8:* Pat Riley is named NBA Coach of the Year.

1998—*April 19:* Heat finish regular season with a 55–27 record and win their second consecutive Atlantic Division title.

1999—*May 5:* Heat end regular season at 33–17, and win the Atlantic Division for third straight year.

—*May 19:* Alonzo Mourning named NBA's Defensive Player of the Year.

2000—*January 2:* The Heat win their inaugural game at the AmericanAirlines Arena with a 111–103 overtime victory over the Orlando Magic.

—*April 19:* Heat end season with 52–30 record and win the Atlantic Division for fourth year in a row.

—*May 21:* After sweeping Detroit 3–0, in opening round of playoffs, the Heat lose to the Knicks, 4–3, in the Eastern Conference Semifinals.

2003—*October:* Pat Riley steps down as head coach, but stays on as president of the Heat.

2004—In Stan Van Gundy's first year as head coach, the Heat go 42–40 and finish second in the Atlantic Division.

—*July:* The Heat acquire all-star center Shaquille O'Neal from the Los Angeles Lakers.

2005—The Heat improve to 59–23 and win the Southeast Division. Riley returns as head coach.

—*June 6:* Season ends when the Detroit Pistons win game seven of the Eastern Conference Finals, 88–82.

2006—*June 20:* Miami Heat win the franchise's first NBA title by defeating the Dallas Mavericks four games to two. Dwyane Wade is named Finals MVP.

After beating Dallas center Erick Dampier to the rim, Dwyane Wade throws down a slam during Game 1 of the 2006 NBA Finals.

ALL ABOARD FOR A CHAMPIONSHIP 1

Great players make great plays, especially in pressure situations. A blocked shot by Miami Heat guard Dwyane Wade against the Detroit Pistons in the 2006 Eastern Conference Finals saved a crucial game for the Heat. Wade's play also kept the Heat on the path toward winning its first NBA title.

In Game 3 of the series, the Heat started off looking like they would cruise to an easy win. They led 49–38 at halftime. After three quarters, Miami led 74–62. Then, the Pistons started the fourth quarter by scoring eleven unanswered points.

The team that had been in command of the game began falling apart. During Detroit's 11–0 run, the Heat missed three shots and four free throws while committing five fouls and three turnovers. With the score 74–73, Pistons forward Antonio McDyess was open for a dunk. The Pistons were poised to take the lead with seven minutes left.

That was when Wade decided to take over. "Guys look at me and say, 'It's your time,'" Wade said. "That's all you need."[1]

Wade blocked the dunk attempt. Eight seconds later he sank a jump shot to give the Heat their first two points of the quarter.

Detroit coach Flip Saunders summed up Wade's game-saving play in four words. "Play of the game," Saunders said.

The Heat went on to outscore the Pistons 22–10 for a 98–83 win and a 2–1 lead in the Eastern Conference Finals. They would go on to defeat the Pistons and then the Dallas Mavericks to win their first NBA title.

In 2002–03, the Miami Heat had been one of the weakest teams in the NBA. That season they went 25–57 and finished seventh in the Atlantic Division. Three years later, they were the best team in the league. A couple of coaching changes and a blockbuster trade made the amazing turnaround possible.

In October 2003, longtime Heat coach Pat Riley resigned. During Riley's eight seasons as head coach, the Heat had gone to the playoffs six times. They had won the Atlantic Division four times, but the Heat had never won an NBA championship. During Riley's last two seasons as head coach, the Heat had played poorly, compiling a record of 61–103.

Riley was replaced by his assistant coach, Stan Van Gundy. Riley's leaving was not unexpected. He said that he had been thinking about leaving for the past two years. Riley thought that the Heat needed a "new voice" and a "new energy."[2] He also thought that Van Gundy was the coach who would bring this new voice and energy.

During Van Gundy's only full season as head coach, Miami improved to 42–40. That was their

Shaq videos, photographs, stats, bio, quiz, quotes, articles, and even his game day diet can be found on the **Shaq Central** Web site.

EDITOR'S CHOICE

first winning season in three years. They also won the first round of the playoffs before losing to the Indiana Pacers in the Eastern Conference Semifinals.

During the off-season, the Heat acquired superstar center Shaquille O'Neal from the Lakers. Riley was serving as the Heat's president when they made the deal. O'Neal was expected to lead the Heat to an NBA championship.

"From junior high on up to the pros, in every single game where I played for a championship, either I was beat because the other team had the big guy, or I won because we had the big guy," Riley said. "I know how important the dominant big man is in the game of basketball."[3]

With the addition of Shaq, the Heat improved to 59–23 in 2004–05. They easily won the Southeast Division and swept the first two rounds of the playoffs. In the opening round, the Heat swept the New Jersey Nets 4–0. They followed that with a four-game sweep of the Washington Wizards. Going into the Eastern Conference Finals against the Detroit Pistons, the Heat had won eleven games in a row.

The Pistons were the defending NBA champions. In the regular season, the Pistons had played the Heat three times and won twice. They wanted to become back-to-back NBA champions like the

3 1833 05294 2536

1988–89 and 1989–90 Pistons. They were not going to let the Heat stop them.

The first two games were on Miami's home court. In Game 1, Shaq returned to action after a bruised thigh had caused him to miss the last two games of the series against Washington. He scored 20 points in 33 minutes but that was not enough to keep the Pistons from winning 90–81. Dwyane Wade was the star of Game 2. His 40 points, 8 rebounds, and 6 assists sparked the Heat to a 92–86 win.

For Games 3 and 4, the series shifted to Detroit. There was another split. Miami won game three, 113–104, but Detroit tied the series with a 106–96 win in game four.

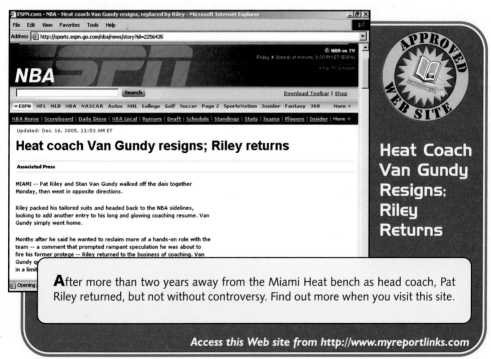

Heat Coach Van Gundy Resigns; Riley Returns

After more than two years away from the Miami Heat bench as head coach, Pat Riley returned, but not without controversy. Find out more when you visit this site.

Access this Web site from http://www.myreportlinks.com

▲ Jack Ramsay is a sportscaster and former Hall of Fame head coach. He first reported that Pat Riley would be returning to coach the Heat.

An 88–76 win in Game 5 put the Heat one win away from going to the NBA Finals. Shaq scored 20 points while Heat reserve forward Rasual Butler came off the bench to score 12 points.

Game 6 turned out to be one of the Heat's all-time worst playoff performances. Wade was out with a rib injury and his offense was sorely missed. Detroit won 91–66. Miami's 66 points was the team's lowest output ever in a playoff game. The Pistons closed out the series with an 88–82 win. The Heat led 79–78 with 1:26 left, but Detroit made 6-of-6 critical free throws late in the game.

The 2004–05 season could have been remembered as one of the Heat's best. But Riley refused to keep the team intact. During the off-season he made a flurry of trades and deals. Four players— Eddie Jones, Damon Jones, Keyon Dooling, and Rasual Butler—were dealt away. They were replaced by Jason Williams, Antoine Walker, Gary Payton, and James Posey.

During the off-season there were also constant rumors and speculation that Riley would return as the Heat's coach. In June 2005, Riley told reporters that he might "take a little bit more of an active participation" in the team.[4] A month later, former Heat broadcaster Jack Ramsay reported on ESPN that Riley would be replacing Van Gundy.

James Posey gets a face full of hands as he battles for a loose ball during the 2006 NBA Finals.

The rumors ended on December 12, 2005, when the Heat hastily called a press conference to announce what had been rumored for months. Stan Van Gundy was resigning and Pat Riley was returning as the head coach of the Miami Heat.

The Heat had gotten off to a slow start. O'Neal was sidelined with a sprained ankle and missed eighteen of the first twenty-one games. When Van Gundy resigned, the Heat had a record of 11–10. Van Gundy said that he wanted to spend more time with his family. Still, there was a strong feeling that Riley wanted him to leave.

At any rate, the Heat showed a marked improvement under Riley. His return to coaching coincided with Shaq's return to the Heat lineup. The Heat went 41–20 the rest of the way and ended the regular season with a 52–30 record. They would begin the playoffs by facing the Chicago Bulls.

The Heat began this series without having Alonzo Mourning to back up Shaq at center. But in Game 1, Shaq played like he did not need anyone to give him a rest. He scored 27 points and grabbed 16 rebounds. Wade added another 30 points and 11 assists to give the Heat a 111–106 win. In Game 2, Jason Williams and Shaq paced Miami with 22 points each. Wade added 21 points and 7 assists in the Heat's 115–108 win.

The Bulls were able to tie the series after they returned to Chicago for Games 3 and 4. Game 3 was one of the worst playoff games of O'Neal's career. He was held to only 8 points. Antoine Walker fouled out and James Posey got a one-game suspension for a flagrant foul during the Bulls' 109–90 win. Despite a 20-point, 10-assist double-double performance by Wade, the Heat also lost Game 4, 93–87.

After the Game 4 letdown, the Heat regrouped and ended the series with back-to-back lopsided

Dwyane Wade was selected fifth overall in the 2003 NBA Draft and began playing for the Heat. He became the only rookie in Heat history to lead the team in scoring average in the postseason. Many other interesting facts about him can be found at **The Official Site of Dwyane Wade.**

EDITOR'S CHOICE

wins. They won Game 5, 92–78, and Game 6, 113–96. In the series finale, Shaq had 30 points, 20 rebounds, and 5 assists. Wade added complementary scoring and playmaking with 23 points and 6 assists.

In the Eastern Conference Semifinals, the Heat had a sloppy opening game against the New Jersey Nets. Poor shooting and a rash of turnovers helped the Nets take a 38–21 lead after one quarter. The Nets went on to post a comfortable 100–88 win. After the loss, O'Neal reminded reporters that he had been down 1–0 in playoff series plenty of times.

"The key is to not have two games in a row like this," Shaq said.[5]

Game 2 was not anything like Game 1. The Heat raced off to an early 41–19 lead and trounced the Nets 111–89. Wade (31 points) and O'Neal (21 points) combined for 52 points. Gary Payton gave the Heat a quick scoring boost with 11 points in fifteen minutes of action.

Games 3 and 4 were in New Jersey, but the Nets did not enjoy any home court advantage. Miami posted nearly identical wins of 103–92 and 102–92. The Heat looked forward to wrapping up the series at home.

In Game 5, Wade showed his knack for making the big play when it mattered most. With one second left, the Nets were trailing 106–105. Guard

▲ Dwyane Wade (left) and Shaquille O'Neal walk off the court after a hard-fought first half of Game 5 of the 2006 NBA Finals.

Jason Kidd was inbounding the ball, and it appeared New Jersey would have one last shot. Wade broke for the ball and intercepted it. That play saved the game and ended the series.

"With one second left, all you want to do is make it tough," Wade said. "And I was able to get there, get my hand on the ball and that was all she wrote."[6]

The Heat had won six of their last seven play-off games, but there was no time for celebrating. They had to face the Detroit Pistons, the same team which had ended the Heat's run for the title one year earlier. Everyone knew that Miami was a good team, but nearly everyone believed that the Pistons were better.

Detroit Coach Flip Saunders believed the series would hinge on stopping Shaq. "He's still the most dominant guy in the game," Saunders said.[7]

O'Neal thought that keeping his teammates involved in the offense was more important than his individual stats. "I'm just playing a smart game," Shaq said after Game 4 against the Nets. "I'm getting it and trying to keep everybody involved. It's an easier game for me when everybody's involved."[8]

For much of Game 1 against Detroit, Shaq and Wade were in foul trouble. Thanks to strong contributions from others, the Heat won 91–86.

Walker, Williams, and Payton combined to score 41 points.

In Game 2, Shaq and Wade stayed out of foul trouble and scored a total of 53 points. Shaq also had 12 rebounds, and Wade had 7. Still, that was not enough to keep the Pistons from getting a 92–88 victory. Detroit forward Tayshaun Prince was a major factor with 24 points and 11 rebounds.

Game 3 saw even more offense from Shaq and Wade. The Heat worked the ball inside to Shaq as much as possible. He finished with 27 points and

For a good overview of the team, including the latest news, player bios, injuries, and standings, visit this **Miami Heat Team Page.** Photographs, team stats, and a summary of recent signings are also provided.

12 rebounds. When the Pistons were able to stop Shaq, Wade would step up his shooting and scoring, and added 35 points. Miami won 98–83.

"We took it upon ourselves to be leaders," Wade said, "and leaders find a way to help their team win."[9]

The same pattern held in Game 4, as Wade's 31 points paced Miami to an 89–78 victory. Detroit avoided elimination with a 91–78 win in Game 5, but the Heat wrapped up the series by winning Game 6, 95–78. A touch of the flu had Wade feeling weak, but he still scored 14 points. Williams scored 21 points, hitting 10 of 12 shots. Yet, it was Shaq who once again put up big numbers in a big game. He scored 28 points and gathered 16 rebounds.

When he first came to Miami in July 2004, Shaq brashly said that he would lead the Heat to an NBA championship. "I'm going to bring a championship to Miami," O'Neal said. "I promise."[10]

Now it was up to him to make good on his vow in the 2006 NBA finals.

The Dallas Mavericks were a dedicated team determined to see that Shaq did not keep his promise. After the first two games of the NBA Finals, it looked like Dallas was going to achieve that goal.

In Game 1, Shaq shot much better from the floor than from the foul line. He sank 8 of 11 from

Heat forward Antoine Walker celebrates after Miami wins the NBA championship.

the floor, but only 1 of 9 free throws. When he got the ball, the Mavs would quickly double- or even triple-team him. That usually forced Shaq to pass the ball off. When he did not pass off, they would exploit his poor foul shooting by putting him on the line. The strategy worked well enough to give the Mavs a 90–80 win.

Game 2 was a repeat of that strategy. By continuing to double- and triple-team Shaq, the Mavs held him to five shots and five points. Shaq continued to struggle at the foul line by only hitting one of seven free throws. After Dallas opened a 74–49 third quarter lead, Shaq sat out the rest of the game. The Mavs cruised to an easy 99–85 win.

Only two teams had won an NBA title after going down 2–0 in the Finals. It was not looking like the Heat would become the third team to do it.

In Game 3, a combination of Wade taking over the game and a Mavs meltdown gave the Heat their first win of the Finals. After three quarters, Dallas had built a 77–68 lead. With 10:56 left, Wade picked up his fifth foul. It seemed like Dallas was in command and well on their way to taking a three games to none lead in the series.

In the final 6:15, though, Dallas only hit 2-of-7 shots and made 5 turnovers. During that span, the Heat outscored them 22–7. A free throw by Dallas's Dirk Nowitzki cut Miami's lead to one with 3.4 seconds left. Nowitzki missed the second

Too hot to handle! Heat win first title - NBA - MSNBC.com - Microsoft Internet Explorer

File   Edit   View   Favorites   Tools   Help

Address http://www.msnbc.msn.com/id/13447388/

NBC

Sports
Scores, Schedules
NFL
College Football
NBA
College Basketball
Baseball
NHL
Golf
NASCAR / Motors
Tennis
Horse Racing
Soccer
Other Sports
Notre Dame Central
Fan Zone
Slide shows
Fantasy Sports
Video
U.S. News
Politics
World N

Too hot to handle! Heat win first NBA title
MVP Wade, Miami edge Mavs in Game 6; Riley, Shaq add to ring collection

Lucy Nicholson / Reuters

Miami Heat players (from left to right) Udonis Haslem, Jason Williams, Dwyane Wade, Gary Payton, Alonzo Mourning, coach Pat Riley (holding trophy), James Posey, Antoine Walker and Shaquille O'Neal pose with

Too Hot to Handle! Heat Win First NBA Title

The 2005–06 season proved to be a historic one for the Miami Heat as they celebrated their first NBA championship in eighteen years as a franchise. They beat the Dallas Mavericks to clinch the trophy. This article offers some franchise highlights and a description of the celebratory parade.

Access this Web site from http://www.myreportlinks.com

free throw and Miami escaped with a 98–96 win. Wade was the leading scorer (42) and rebounder (13) in Game 3.

"He's just fabulous," Shaq said. "He's a great one. And he's so young with a lot of room to improve. It's going to be fun to watch him."[11]

Game 4 found O'Neal and his teammates having more fun watching Wade dazzle. Despite playing with a sore knee, Wade lit it up with a 36-point, 6-rebound performance. Wade's scoring was also making it easier for the Heat to work the ball inside to Shaq, who responded with 17 points and 13 rebounds. The Heat tied the series with a convincing 98–74 win.

Game 5 was the only game of the Finals to go into overtime. Once again, Wade was the hero in a Heat victory. With 9.1 seconds left, the Heat trailed 100–99. During a timeout, Coach Riley decided that Wade would be the go-to guy in that crucial situation.

"Besides Dwyane," Riley said after the game, "we did not have a second option."[12]

Wade dribbled his way around and through four Dallas defenders before being fouled by Nowitzki with 1.9 seconds left. Then he calmly sank two free throws to give the Heat a 101–100 victory.

The momentum had clearly shifted to Miami. Losing three in a row on the Heat's home court put the Mavs one game away from elimination. Game 6 at the American Airlines Center in Dallas turned into a must win for the Mavs.

Heat coach Pat Riley approached Game 6 expecting it to be the last game of the season. He only packed one tie, one suit, and one dress shirt for the trip to Dallas. He did not believe that a Game 7 would be needed.

Riley was right. Wade was close to unstoppable while Shaq, Udonis Haslem, and Antoine Walker kept coming through with timely scoring and rebounding. The end result was a 95–92 win for the Heat.

O'Neal, Haslem, and Walker combined for 43 points and 33 rebounds in the decisive Game 6. Wade's 36 points and 10 rebounds in Game 6 ensured his selection as the Finals MVP. In Miami's four wins, Wade averaged just over 39 points a game.

In the midst of the team celebration, Shaq revealed that he promised a championship because he expected great things from Wade.

"I made that [championship] promise because of D-Wade," O'Neal said. "I knew he was a special player."[13]

Winners never get tired of winning. For Coach Riley, it was the fifth time that he had coached an NBA championship team, but it had been eighteen years since he had done it. That lengthy interval set an NBA record. He hinted that he could either be done chasing championships, or go after number six.

"After eighteen years, you keep chasing it and chasing it,' Riley said. "This gives me a sense of absolute freedom from having to chase it, desperately chase it."[14]

Whether Coach Riley, Shaq, Wade, and the Heat will win another title, no one knows. But, there is little doubt that the Heat should continue to be one of the NBA's elite teams for years to come.

27

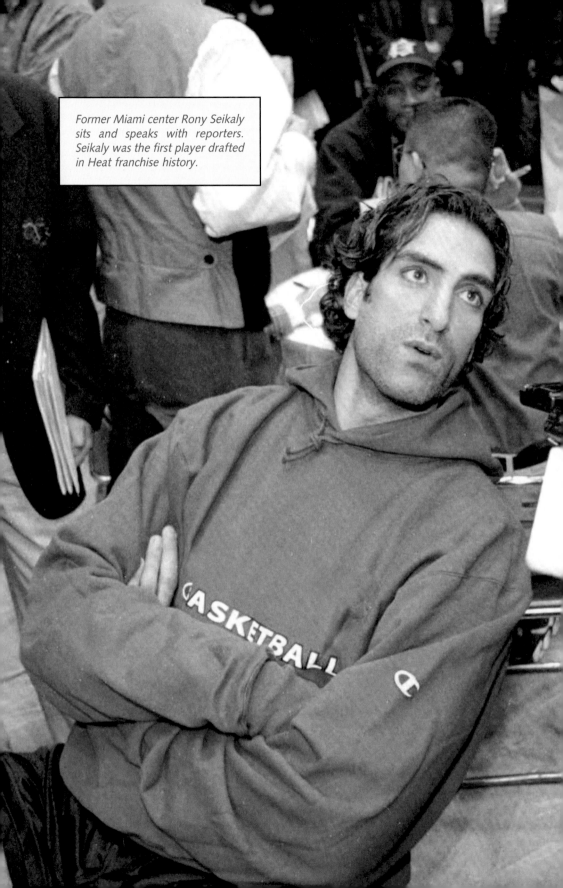

Former Miami center Rony Seikaly sits and speaks with reporters. Seikaly was the first player drafted in Heat franchise history.

1988–1995

(2)

In the 1980s, the NBA made one of the most remarkable comebacks in the history of professional sports. During the 1970s, attendance, interest, and television ratings dwindled. That changed after college stars Magic Johnson (Michigan State) and Larry Bird (Indiana State) became pros. When Johnson and Bird faced off in the 1979 NCAA championship game, it became the most watched championship game in NCAA history.

Michigan State won 75–64, but the big winner was the NBA. Bird joined the Boston Celtics, and Johnson skipped his final two years of college to play for the Los Angeles Lakers. From 1980 to 1989, either the Lakers or Celtics advanced to the championship round of the NBA playoffs. The Lakers won five NBA titles in that ten-year span, and the Celtics won three.

Three times in that decade there was a huge worldwide audience to watch a Los Angeles versus Boston matchup for the title, with the Lakers winning two-of-three. Fan interest was reaching an all-time high. Satellite broadcasts were beaming NBA games into countries and continents that had previously shown little interest in pro basketball. The NBA decided to cash in on its greatly expanding popularity by adding some new teams.

Things Warming Up in the Sunshine State

There were investors in Miami who wanted to land an NBA franchise, but the city did not have a great reputation for being a sports town. Miami once had a franchise in the American Basketball Association (ABA). But after two seasons of poor attendance, the Miami Floridians were forced to play some of their home games in other Florida cities. The NFL's Miami Dolphins and the University of Miami Hurricanes produced championship football teams, but not all of their home games were sellouts at the cavernous Orange Bowl.

Nevertheless, investors Billy Cunningham, Zev Bufman, and Ted Arison firmly believed that Miamians would strongly support an NBA team. The three investors came from very different backgrounds. Cunningham was the only one with a solid background in pro basketball. He had played in the NBA and the ABA from 1965 to 1976, and

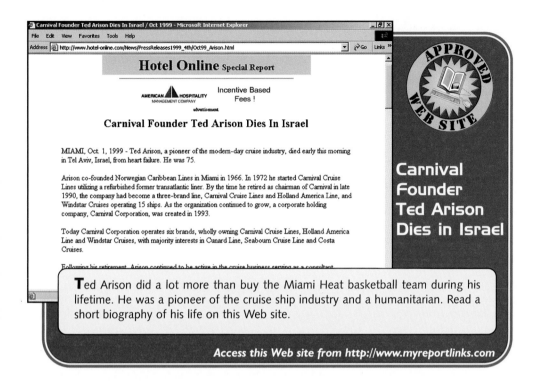

Carnival Founder Ted Arison Dies In Israel / Oct 1999 - Microsoft Internet Explorer

File   Edit   View   Favorites   Tools   Help

Address   http://www.hotel-online.com/News/PressReleases1999_4th/Oct99_Arison.html   Go   Links »

Hotel Online Special Report

AMERICAN HOSPITALITY
MANAGEMENT COMPANY

Incentive Based
Fees !

advertisement

Carnival Founder Ted Arison Dies In Israel

MIAMI, Oct. 1, 1999 - Ted Arison, a pioneer of the modern-day cruise industry, died early this morning in Tel Aviv, Israel, from heart failure. He was 75.

Arison co-founded Norwegian Caribbean Lines in Miami in 1966. In 1972 he started Carnival Cruise Lines utilizing a refurbished former transatlantic liner. By the time he retired as chairman of Carnival in late 1990, the company had become a three-brand line, Carnival Cruise Lines and Holland America Line, and Windstar Cruises operating 15 ships. As the organization continued to grow, a corporate holding company, Carnival Corporation, was created in 1993.

Today Carnival Corporation operates six brands, wholly owning Carnival Cruise Lines, Holland America Line and Windstar Cruises, with majority interests in Cunard Line, Seabourn Cruise Line and Costa Cruises.

Following his retirement, Arison continued to be active in the cruise business serving as a consultant.

Carnival Founder Ted Arison Dies in Israel

Ted Arison did a lot more than buy the Miami Heat basketball team during his lifetime. He was a pioneer of the cruise ship industry and a humanitarian. Read a short biography of his life on this Web site.

Access this Web site from http://www.myreportlinks.com

was named to the NBA's 50th Anniversary All-Time Team as one of the fifty greatest players in the history of the league. Cunningham had also coached the Philadelphia 76ers to an NBA title in 1983.

Bufman made his fortune producing Broadway plays and musicals. He did not have a strong sports background, but he had the business experience and connections to help Miami get an NBA franchise.

Arison had founded the highly successful Miami-based Carnival Cruise Lines. That had made him wealthy enough to become a major investor and prominent factor in bringing pro basketball to Miami.

⊜ Officially a Franchise

In June 1986, Cunningham and Bufman formally applied for an NBA franchise. Ten months later, the NBA announced the addition of four new teams to the league—Miami, Charlotte, Minnesota, and Orlando. Miami and Charlotte would begin play during the 1988–89 season. Orlando and Minnesota would join the league one year later. To help ensure the financial stability of the new franchises, the NBA mandated that all four teams had to sell ten thousand season tickets before they could begin play.

After meeting that goal, the Heat were ready to begin drafting and signing players. As the Heat's general manager, Cunningham decided to go with younger players instead of seasoned veterans.

"The first step was the decision not to go with older players, for the simple reason that we had to be bad before we could be good. . . . We knew that we'd take our lumps early," Cunningham said. "And we'd have to have patience and live through some tough times and hopefully not make many mistakes when we got to the draft."[1]

⊜ The First Players

The Heat's first two draft picks—center Rony Seikaly from Syracuse University and guard Kevin Edwards from DePaul—became starters. Their third pick—forward Grant Long from Eastern

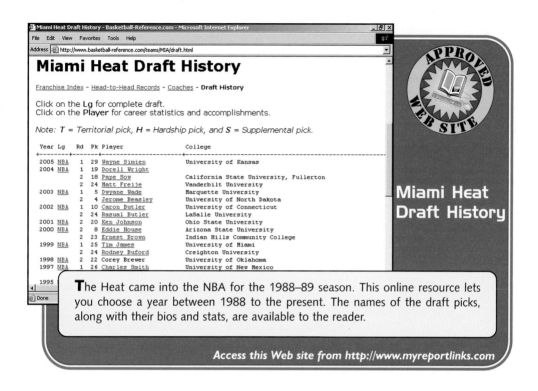

Miami Heat Draft History

Franchise Index - Head-to-Head Records - Coaches - **Draft History**

Click on the **Lg** for complete draft.
Click on the **Player** for career statistics and accomplishments.

Note: *T* = Territorial pick, *H* = Hardship pick, and *S* = Supplemental pick.

Year	Lg	Rd	Pk	Player	College
2005	NBA	1	29	Wayne Simien	University of Kansas
2004	NBA	1	19	Dorell Wright	
		2	18	Pape Sow	California State University, Fullerton
		2	24	Matt Freije	Vanderbilt University
2003	NBA	1	5	Dwyane Wade	Marquette University
		2	4	Jerome Beasley	University of North Dakota
2002	NBA	1	10	Caron Butler	University of Connecticut
		2	24	Rasual Butler	LaSalle University
2001	NBA	2	20	Ken Johnson	Ohio State University
2000	NBA	2	8	Eddie House	Arizona State University
		2	23	Ernest Brown	Indian Hills Community College
1999	NBA	1	25	Tim James	University of Miami
		2	24	Rodney Buford	Creighton University
1998	NBA	2	22	Corey Brewer	University of Oklahoma
1997	NBA	1	26	Charles Smith	University of New Mexico
1995					

Miami Heat Draft History

The Heat came into the NBA for the 1988–89 season. This online resource lets you choose a year between 1988 to the present. The names of the draft picks, along with their bios and stats, are available to the reader.

Access this Web site from http://www.myreportlinks.com

Michigan—was a starter in all but nine games during Miami's first season. To mold these untested college players into effective pros, the Heat hired Ron Rothstein as their first head coach.

Rothstein had been an assistant coach with Detroit and hoped to build a team based on strong defensive principles. He knew that the first season would be difficult, so he did not try to predict how many games the first-year expansion team would win.

A Tough Start

As expected, the wins did not come right away. The Heat set an NBA record for early-season futility by losing their first seventeen games. On December 14, 1988, the Heat's lengthy losing streak ended with a 89–88 win over the L.A. Clippers. Their longest winning streak that season was a three-game spurt in late March. Miami finished the year 15–67.

Comedians and sports commentators made jokes about the Heat, but their loyal fans stuck by them. Thirty-five of their forty-one home games were sellouts, and some savvy observers of the NBA asserted that Miami was doing okay for a first-year team.

NBA Commissioner David Stern reminded skeptical fans and followers that building a winning team in the NBA was a gradual process. "Right now it looks dark for Miami," Stern admitted. "But everything takes time. They have no place to go but up, and up they will go."[2]

Signs of Improvement

In their second season, the Heat did go up a little bit. Their first two draft picks—Glen Rice from Michigan and Sherman Douglas from Syracuse—gave the Heat some additional offense they had been lacking. That made it easier for center Rony Seikaly to get open shots. Seikaly averaged 16.6 points per game and won the NBA's Most Improved Player Award. Douglas was named to the NBA's All-Rookie First Team and Rice was chosen for the All-Rookie Second Team.

Find the latest news from around the league on **NBA.com**, the official Web site of the NBA. You will be able to learn about the league's history, teams, players, and more.

EDITOR'S CHOICE

Still, the individual honors did not translate into many more wins for the Heat. They finished the season with an 18–64 record. Only a 17–65 record by the New Jersey Nets kept the Heat from having the worst record in the NBA. Despite having an 11–30 home record, the Heat sold out all of their forty-one home games. The wins were slow in coming, but their fan base remained strong.

During their third season, the Heat showed only a slight improvement. They won 24 games and lost 58. Cunningham expected them to do

NBA.com Ron Rothstein - Microsoft Internet Explorer

File   Edit   View   Favorites   Tools   Help

Address http://www.nba.com/coachfile/ron_rothstein/index.html?nav=page   Go   Links »

NBA   GLOBAL   D-LEAGUE   WNBA   Members Sign In Join Now

TEAMS   PLAYERS   SCORES   STANDINGS   STATS   SCHEDULE   TICKETS   PHOTOS   NEWS   FANTASY   M

NBA Coaches

COACHES   TOOLS

Ron Rothstein
TOOLS   Print   E-mail   RSS Feeds   E-News Sign Up

College - Rhode Island

A quick look at his resume will tell you that Ron Rothstein has enjoyed a
great deal of success in all levels of the game of basketball from high school
to the professional ranks. A resume which is highlighted by over 40 years in
the game, Rothstein brings a wealth of experience and knowledge as he
serves his third stint with the HEAT organization. The 2005-06 season marks
Rothstein's 26th season of involvement in the NBA. Beginning as a regional
scout in 1979, Rothstein has served as a head coach twice in the NBA, an
assistant coach with five different franchises, as a regional scout with three
teams and also spent one season as an NBA television analyst. During his
17 years on an NBA bench his teams have captured two divisional
championships, and made ten postseason appearances, highlighted by four
Eastern Conference Finals appearances, one Eastern Conference
championship and an NBA Finals appearance in 1988.

Ron Rothstein was the first head coach of the Miami Heat. This online bio
lets you read more about his coaching career which ranged from high school
and college ball to the professional ranks.

better and he felt it was time for a coaching
change. Rothstein resigned after the season ended
and was replaced by veteran NBA coach Kevin
Loughery. Of his time in Miami, Rothstein said,
"As we talked, it became very apparent to me
how draining this thing has been to me and my
family."[3]

Loughery had thorough knowledge of the
game. He had played in the NBA for eleven seasons and had coached in both the NBA and ABA
from 1973 to 1988. Loughery felt that he was

inheriting a team that was long on talent, but short on desire.

Building a Winner

That season, the Heat took the court with a more positive attitude. The players expected to win instead of trying not to lose. Seikaly and Rice were now experienced pros instead of raw rookies. In April, Rice was named NBA Player of the Month. Seikaly averaged over 16 points and 11 rebounds a game over the course of the season.

Miami's backcourt also had a new look to go with the team's new attitude. First-round draft pick Steve Smith from Michigan State used his six-foot eight-inch size at the point guard position to give Miami additional offense and rebounding. Smith was also chipping in just over 4 assists per game with his precision passes. Brian Shaw joined the team in January 1992 and performed capably at the other guard position.

The Heat started strong by winning seven of their first ten games. They finished the season with a record of 38–44 and made the playoffs as the eighth-seeded team in the Eastern Conference. They became the first of the NBA's late 1980s expansion teams to qualify for postseason play.

Unfortunately, they had to play the league's defending champions—the Chicago Bulls, led by Michael Jordan. After losing the first two games to

▲ Steve Smith (left) was a Heat first-round draft pick that joined the team prior to the 1991–92 season. He came back to the team to finish his career in 2005. He is horsing around with Udonis Haslem as Shaquille O'Neal looks on.

Chicago, the Heat returned to Miami. They raised hopes of upsetting the Bulls in Game 3 by outscoring them in the first half, 56–51, but Chicago's superior talent prevailed. Michael Jordan's 56-point performance led the Bulls to a 119–114 win and a 3–0 sweep.

Loughery acknowledged that he had lost to a superior team, but he thought that their first playoff appearance would build a foundation for a brighter future.

A Drop-Off

The 1992–93 season began with high hopes, but the Heat's performance never lived up to the expectations. Smith missed the start of the season because of a knee injury, and he only played in forty-eight games. At midseason, the Heat were 14–27, and things never got much better. The team finished the year 36–46 and missed the playoffs.

Miami's fans continued to be patient and supportive, but now some of them were wondering if the team was headed in the right direction. After five seasons in the NBA, the club could not blame their losses on inexperience.

Over .500

Things did not look good when the Heat began the 1993–94 season with a sluggish 3–6 start. Then,

Seikaly, Rice, and Smith began showing some improved scoring ability. That season, they combined to average over 53 points a game. Miami finished the year 42–40. For the first time, the Miami Heat finished the year with a winning record.

The Heat enjoyed another franchise first that season. They averaged 103.4 points per game while holding their opponents to an average of 100.7. In their five previous seasons, they had always given up more points than they scored.

For the second time in three years, the Heat qualified for the playoffs. Once again, they would be the eighth-seeded team playing the top-seeded team. This time they would be facing the Atlanta

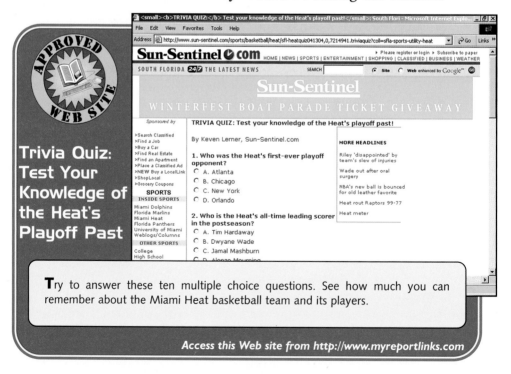

Trivia Quiz: Test Your Knowledge of the Heat's Playoff Past

Try to answer these ten multiple choice questions. See how much you can remember about the Miami Heat basketball team and its players.

Access this Web site from http://www.myreportlinks.com

Hawks, who had won the Central Division with a record of 57–25.

After three games, it looked as if the Heat might pull off a major upset. They had a two games to one lead over Atlanta. One more win would send them to the next round of postseason play. Game 4 would be played before a sellout crowd at Miami Arena. The Heat had the momentum and the home court advantage.

The Hawks responded to the challenge with a 103–89 win. They followed that up with a 102–91 clincher on their home court. The playoff loss led to some major personnel changes by the Heat.

Big Changes

Billy Cunningham's share of the team was bought out by the Arison family. Then, two days before the start of the 1994–95 season, the Heat traded Rony Seikaly to the Golden State Warriors for guard/forward Billy Owens and reserve guard Sasha Danilovic. Five days later, Steve Smith and Grant Long were dealt to the Atlanta Hawks for forward/center Kevin Willis and a future first-round draft pick.

The Heat were starting the season by piecing together a lineup that had spent little time playing and practicing together. And not surprisingly, they started off by losing seven of their first eight games. By mid-season, the Heat were 17–29 and ownership decided that a coaching change was needed.

Ted Arison's son, Mickey, had taken over as the team's majority owner. One day after taking over, Arison hired Dave Wohl as the Heat's executive vice-president of basketball operations. Wohl's first personnel move was to fire head coach Kevin Loughery and replace him with assistant coach Alvin Gentry. "I just didn't like the direction we were heading," Wohl said. "And I didn't want Kevin's status to linger."[4]

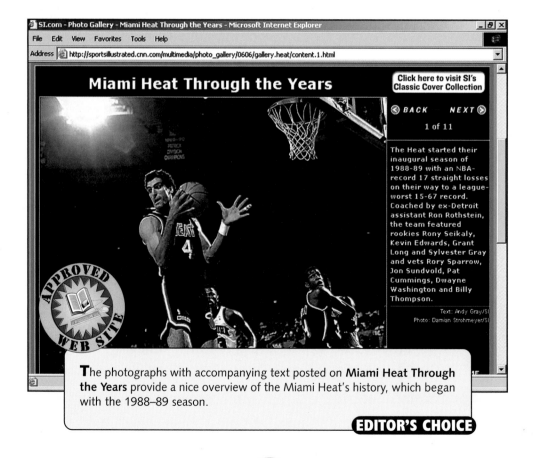

The photographs with accompanying text posted on **Miami Heat Through the Years** provide a nice overview of the Miami Heat's history, which began with the 1988–89 season.

EDITOR'S CHOICE

Gentry was grateful for the opportunity to become an NBA head coach, but it was an uncomfortable situation replacing the man who had hired him. "Kevin hired me here, and I feel very much a sense of loyalty to him," Gentry said. "It's a golden opportunity for me, but yet it was a very, very tough situation seeing Kevin leave."[5]

A Big Step Back

Usually, changing coaches that late in the season does not make much difference in a team's performance. That was the case with the Heat. Under Gentry, they went 15–21 and ended the season with a 32–50 record.

"We had a talented team," recalled Glen Rice. "Myself, Kevin Willis, Bimbo Coles, Billy Owens— but we played under our potential. After making the playoffs and finishing better than .500 in 1993–94, we took a big step back in 1994–95 . . ."[6]

After seven seasons, it seemed as though the Heat were back where they started when they joined the NBA. Their fans were getting impatient and it was time for some major changes. Those major changes would begin when the Heat hired one of the NBA's best known and most successful coaches.

1995–2000

3

For almost four months in 1995, the Miami Heat basketball team was like a ship without a captain. In early April, they announced that Alvin Gentry would not be returning as head coach. While their fans waited and wondered about who was going to lead the team, Heat executives were quietly working out a deal to lure Pat Riley away from his head coaching position with the New York Knicks.

Coach Pat Riley

Riley is clearly one of the most successful and high profile coaches in the history of the NBA. He won four NBA championships while coaching the Los Angeles Lakers from 1981 to 1990. During that time, the Lakers won the Pacific Division title nine years in a row.

After Riley left the Lakers to coach the Knicks, New York won the Atlantic Division two years in a row and finished second once. Although the Knicks failed to capture the NBA championship, Riley's name was still synonymous with winning. In thirteen seasons as an NBA coach, Riley had never failed to get his team into the playoffs.

The Heat agreed to pay Riley $3 million per year, and give him complete control of their basketball operations. He also received enough stock in the franchise to give him an ownership interest. Miami gave Riley two different job titles—team president and head coach. The Heat also had to compensate the Knicks for the loss of Riley. Miami

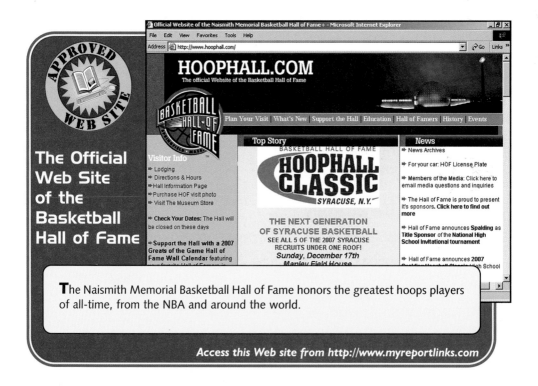

The Official Web Site of the Basketball Hall of Fame

The Naismith Memorial Basketball Hall of Fame honors the greatest hoops players of all-time, from the NBA and around the world.

Access this Web site from http://www.myreportlinks.com

gave the Knicks its first-round draft pick in 1996 and one million dollars.

Under Riley, the Heat kicked off the 1995–96 season with an impressive 11–3 start, but they could not maintain that pace. By midseason, they had a sub-par record of 18–23. Fans were concerned because the Heat had acquired two all-star caliber players in the form of center Alonzo Mourning and point guard Tim Hardaway. The Heat finished the year, 42–40, and barely made it into the playoffs as the Eastern Conference's eighth-seeded team.

Messing With the Bulls, Getting the Horns

Once again, the Heat would have to face the Eastern Conference champion in the first round of the playoffs. The Chicago Bulls set a new league record that season by winning 72 games and only losing 10. Michael Jordan was the team's peerless superstar, but his teammates Scottie Pippen, Dennis Rodman, Steve Kerr, and Toni Kukoc had worked together to make the Bulls the best team in the league.

Chicago had no trouble sweeping Miami in three straight games. Riley did not offer any excuses. He admitted that they were beaten by a much better team. About all he could do was ask Heat fans to be patient while he worked to assemble an improved team for the 1996–97 season.

New Additions

In the off-season, Riley bolstered the team by signing a pair of free agents: six-foot six-inch guard/forward "Thunder" Dan Majerle and six-foot eleven-inch forward P. J. Brown. Majerle's ability to play two positions and his fearless hard-nosed style of play made him a valuable addition to the Heat. Along with playing scrappy defense, Majerle would routinely dive to the floor to grab loose balls.

Former teammate Kurt Rambis praised Majerle by saying, "You couldn't ask for a better guy in the locker room or a better guy, a better companion out there on the floor when you're going to war. "[1]

Brown was best known for his strong defense, but he could also be counted on to average 10 points and grab about 8 rebounds per game.

After a disappointing 5–4 start, the Heat won nineteen of their next twenty-two games. Fans were flocking back to Miami Arena and the Heat's average attendance for home games exceeded fifteen thousand. In mid-season, Riley engineered a trade that brought six-foot eight-inch forward Jamal Mashburn to Miami. Mashburn joined the team on the tail end of an eleven-game winning streak.

Division Champs

The Heat ended the 1996–97 regular season with a 61–21 record, the best in the history of the

▲ Jamal Mashburn of the Miami Heat struggles with Kings center Vlade Divac for possession of the ball during this game in 1999.

franchise. Throughout the season, they played superb defense by holding their opponents to only 89.3 points per game. They easily won the Atlantic Division. For the first time, the Heat would be entering the playoffs as a top-seeded team, instead of an eighth-seeded one.

⊜1997 Playoffs

In the opening round of the playoffs, the Heat faced the Orlando Magic. Miami easily won the first two games by an average margin of 26 points. Orlando then turned it around with back-to-back home court victories. Anfernee Hardaway kept Orlando's hopes alive by scoring 83 points in those wins. Then, the Heat closed out the series with a 91–83 win. For the first time, the Heat would be advancing to the second round of the playoffs.

Round two matched the Heat up against the Knicks. Coach Riley would be facing the team that he left so he could come to Miami. New York took command early by winning three of the first four games. Game 5 was marred by a bench-clearing brawl that began after the Heat had the game wrapped up. After being undercut by the Knicks' Charlie Ward, P. J. Brown slammed him to the floor.

Brown's retaliation earned him a two-game suspension, but the Heat were able to win without him. They moved on to play their old playoff nemesis, Chicago, for the Eastern Conference title.

⊖Another Bullfight

Michael Jordan and the Chicago Bulls continued their playoff dominance over Miami. Chicago opened with two consecutive wins over the Heat at the United Center. After the series moved to Miami, the Bulls trounced the Heat 98–74 in Game 3. The Heat held on by eking out an 87–80 win in Game 4, but the Bulls wrapped it up back home with a convincing 100–87 win in Game 5. Miami ended a promising season by losing their last three home games.

Although it ended on a losing note, 1996–97 was the most successful season to date in the Heat's short history. Riley was named the NBA's

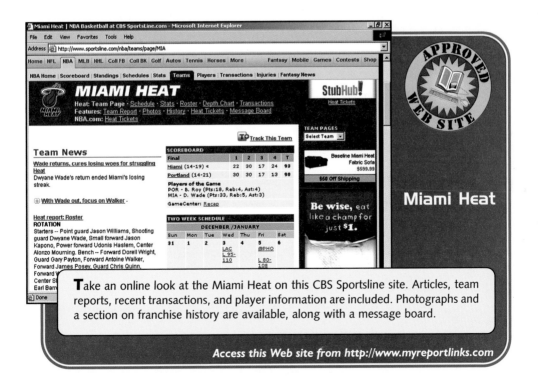

Take an online look at the Miami Heat on this CBS Sportsline site. Articles, team reports, recent transactions, and player information are included. Photographs and a section on franchise history are available, along with a message board.

Access this Web site from http://www.myreportlinks.com

Coach of the Year. He became the first coach in league history to receive that award with three different franchises. Reserve forward Ike Austin became the second Heat player to win the league's Most Improved Player Award, and P. J. Brown was named to the NBA's All-Defensive Second Team. Still, for many Heat fans that was not enough to make up for being routed by the Bulls in the Eastern Conference Finals.

⊖Another Good Year

The 1997–98 season began badly when Mourning was put on the injured list two days before their season opener. Fortunately, Austin did a good job filling in. Mourning returned to the lineup after missing the first twenty-two games. By then, the Heat were 15–7 and well on their way to winning another Atlantic Division championship.

In February, the Heat began a ten-game winning streak which improved their record to 41–18. They posted an impressive 13–2 mark that month, and Riley was named Coach of the Month.

Miami finished the season 55–27, twelve games ahead of the New York Knicks and the New Jersey Nets who tied for second place. That earned the Heat the second seed in the opening round of the playoffs. The Heat would face the seventh-seeded Knicks. During the regular season,

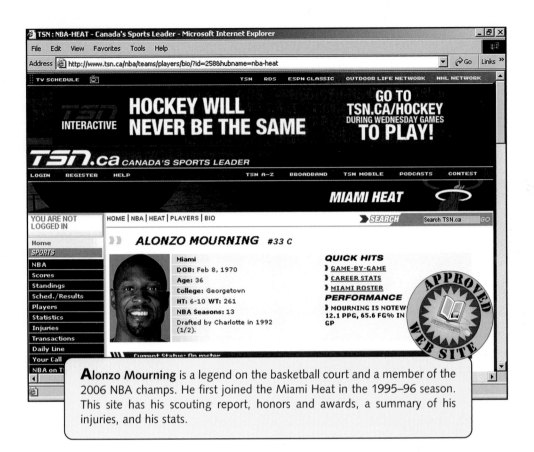

TSN : NBA-HEAT - Canada's Sports Leader - Microsoft Internet Explorer

File   Edit   View   Favorites   Tools   Help

Address http://www.tsn.ca/nba/teams/players/bio/?id=258&hubname=nba-heat

TV SCHEDULE   TSN   RDS   ESPN CLASSIC   OUTDOOR LIFE NETWORK   NHL NETWORK

HOCKEY WILL NEVER BE THE SAME

INTERACTIVE

GO TO TSN.CA/HOCKEY DURING WEDNESDAY GAMES TO PLAY!

TSN.ca CANADA'S SPORTS LEADER

LOGIN   REGISTER   HELP   TSN A-Z   BROADBAND   TSN MOBILE   PODCASTS   CONTEST

MIAMI HEAT

YOU ARE NOT LOGGED IN

HOME | NBA | HEAT | PLAYERS | BIO   SEARCH   Search TSN.ca   GO

Home
SPORTS
NBA
Scores
Standings
Sched./Results
Players
Statistics
Injuries
Transactions
Daily Line
Your Call
NBA on T:

ALONZO MOURNING #33 C

Miami
DOB: Feb 8, 1970
Age: 36
College: Georgetown
HT: 6-10 **WT:** 261
NBA Seasons: 13
Drafted by Charlotte in 1992 (1/2).

QUICK HITS
GAME-BY-GAME
CAREER STATS
MIAMI ROSTER
PERFORMANCE
MOURNING IS NOTEW
12.1 PPG, 65.6 FG% IN
GP

APPROVED WEB SITE

Current Status: On roster

Alonzo Mourning is a legend on the basketball court and a member of the 2006 NBA champs. He first joined the Miami Heat in the 1995–96 season. This site has his scouting report, honors and awards, a summary of his injuries, and his stats.

the Heat and Knicks had played four games with each team winning two.

Even though the Heat had a much better record, they were not heavy favorites. The Knicks had an added incentive to beat Miami. They wanted to once again show Riley that the team he left was superior to the one he joined.

Miami won two of the first three contests, and in Game 4 they were tied 47–47 at halftime. But after three quarters, they trailed the Knicks 71–64, and would lose 90–85. In the waning seconds of a

Heat forward Kevin Willis dunks on Nets forward P. J. Brown. Both Willis and Brown played for the Miami Heat at various points in their careers.

very emotional game, Mourning and New York forward Larry Johnson began throwing punches. Both players were ejected and suspended for the decisive Game 5.

P. J. Brown replaced Mourning at center for Game 5 and had an impressive double-double performance of 18 points and 10 rebounds. Yet, that was not enough to keep the Knicks from outshooting, outrebounding, and outscoring the Heat enroute to a 98–81 win. For the second year in a row, the Heat's playoff hopes ended with a home-court loss. Heat fans began wondering if their team was jinxed and if things would ever change.

Shortened Year

The 1998–99 season was the shortest one in NBA history. The players and management failed to agree on a new collective bargaining agreement after the old one expired. As a result, the players were locked out of their preseason training camps and the season did not begin until February.

In spite of the long layoff, the Heat players were ready when the season finally began. Miami jumped off to an 18–5 start and finished with a 33–17 record. They easily won their third consecutive Atlantic Division title.

Alonzo Mourning enjoyed the best season of his career. He averaged a double-double—20.1

points and 11 rebounds a game. Mourning also led the NBA in blocked shots and was honored as the NBA's Defensive Player of the Year. P. J. Brown was named to the league's All-Defensive Second Team and Hardaway was selected to the All-NBA Second Team.

The Heat averaged 89 points a game while holding their opponents to an average of 84. Heat fans expected their top-seeded team to go deep into the playoffs. An NBA title looked like an attainable goal.

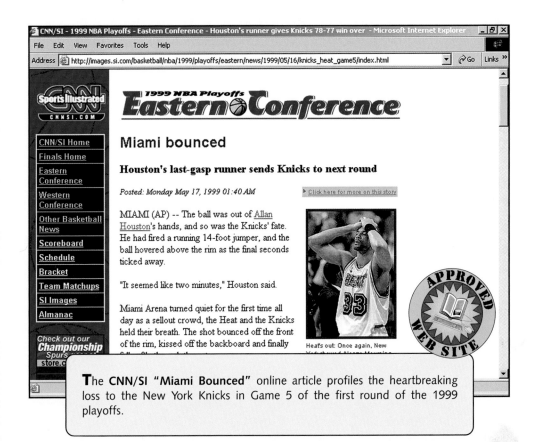

The **CNN/SI "Miami Bounced"** online article profiles the heartbreaking loss to the New York Knicks in Game 5 of the first round of the 1999 playoffs.

For the second year in a row, the Heat had to play the Knicks in the opening round of the playoffs. A 27–23 record and a fourth place finish in the Atlantic Division made the Knicks an eighth-seeded team. Miami was the clear favorite.

High Hopes

The two fierce rivals split the first four games of the best-of-five series. In Game 5, the Knicks broke the Heat's heart with one of the NBA's most famous fantastic finishes.

With 0.8 seconds left in Game 5, Knicks guard Allan Houston launched a running 14-foot jump shot. His soft shot bounced off the rim, then nudged the backboard before falling through the net.

A sellout crowd of 15,200 sat in stunned silence. The Heat got one final shot, but Terry Porter's desperation forty-foot heave was off the mark. For the third year in a row, the Heat's season ended with a home-court playoff loss.

"This one obviously hurts us a lot more than last year," coach Riley said. "Life in basketball has a lot of suffering in it, and we will suffer this one."[2]

Alonzo Mourning expressed the combination of disbelief and anger that the Heat players and fans felt after the incredible loss:

"For it to come down to that kind of shot makes you angry a little bit," Mourning said. "Regardless of the outcome, I still feel that we're a better team than they are."[3]

⊜ New Home

A new century saw the Heat playing in a new arena. On January 2, 2000, Miami played its first game in the ultramodern AmericanAirlines Arena. Miami inaugurated its new home with a 111–103 overtime win over the Orlando Magic. That victory improved their record to 20–9 and the Heat went on to win the Atlantic Division for the fourth year in a row. For the second consecutive season, Alonzo Mourning was the NBA's Defensive Player of the Year after leading the league in blocked shots.

Following a 52–30 regular-season record, the Heat swept the Pistons, three games to none, in the opening round of the Eastern Divisional playoffs. There was no time for celebrating after a first round sweep. Once again, the Knicks stood in Miami's way.

New York was a much better team in 1999–2000. They were second in the Atlantic Division with a 50–32 record. Yet, the Heat had beaten them three out of four games in the regular season. There was hope that a new century would bring more successful playoff results for the Heat.

The 2000 Eastern Conference Semifinals between Miami and New York was one of the most closely contested series in NBA history. Three of the seven games were decided by two points or less. The biggest margin of victory was a 91–83 win by the Knicks in Game 4.

For the frustrated Heat fans the final result was a combination of disappointment and déjà vu. Three years in a row, their season had ended in the same shocking fashion.

Once again the Knicks terminated Miami's postseason hopes with a one-point road win before a stunned sellout crowd. It was a third straight season of failure for the Miami Heat and their fans.

This time, some of the Heat players and most of their fans turned their anger and displeasure to

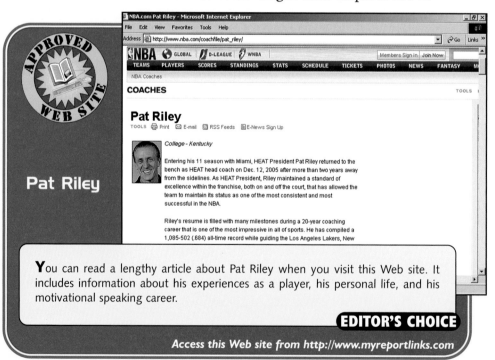

Pat Riley

You can read a lengthy article about Pat Riley when you visit this Web site. It includes information about his experiences as a player, his personal life, and his motivational speaking career.

EDITOR'S CHOICE

Access this Web site from http://www.myreportlinks.com

the officials. Among the players, Jamal Mashburn was the most vocal. "They had three officials in their pocket," Mashburn said. "No blame to them. We had chances to win the thing. But they were terrible."[4]

What would really be terrible for the Heat would be the next few seasons. No one knew it then, but things were going to get a lot worse before they got better.

Miami guard Eddie Jones dribbles past Ben Wallace of the Detroit Pistons.

2000–2004

4

About five months after their disappointing playoff loss to the Knicks, the Heat suffered another big setback. In October 2000, they announced that their all-star center, Alonzo Mourning, had been stricken with a serious kidney disease and was projected to miss the entire 2000–01 season.

Mourning was the heart and soul of the Heat's unyielding defense. For the previous two seasons he had not only been the NBA's Defensive Player of the Year, but also the league leader in blocked shots. Miami no longer had Ike Austin as a backup center. They had traded him to the Los Angeles Clippers in 1998. Miami was forced to go with little used reserve Duane Causwell as their starting center.

Riley had also traded away starters P. J. Brown and Jamal Mashburn. The Heat would be beginning the season with a starting five who had not played together very much. That lack of experience showed when Miami got off to a very poor 5–9 start. In December, the Heat enjoyed a big turnaround by going 12–5. Riley was once again named the NBA's Coach of the Month.

Turning the Season Around

Miami continued their winning ways in January by going 10–4. After a shaky start, the Heat closed out the season finishing second in the Atlantic Division with a 50–32 record. For the

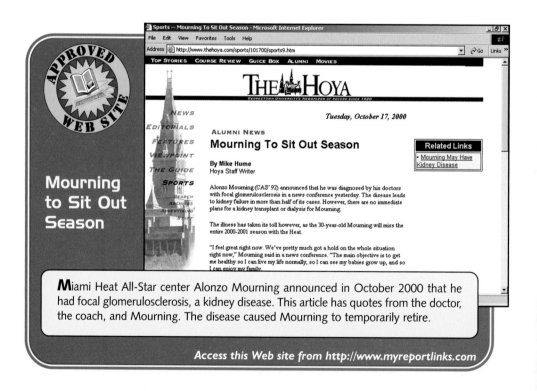

Miami Heat All-Star center Alonzo Mourning announced in October 2000 that he had focal glomerulosclerosis, a kidney disease. This article has quotes from the doctor, the coach, and Mourning. The disease caused Mourning to temporarily retire.

Access this Web site from http://www.myreportlinks.com

sixth consecutive season, the Heat would be going to the playoffs. By the time the season ended, Mourning had returned eager for the post-season.

In the opening round of the playoffs, the third-seeded Heat faced the sixth-seeded Charlotte Hornets. Charlotte's 46–36 record had earned them a third place finish in the Central Division. During the regular season, the Heat had a 2–2 record against the Hornets. Once again, the Heat enjoyed the home court advantage. If the series went to five games, three would be played in Miami.

As it turned out, a fifth game was not needed. Neither was a fourth. For the first time in five years, the Heat were swept in a playoff series.

In Game 1, Miami played before a playoff record crowd of 20,085. In that game, Miami set another playoff record—the most lopsided playoff loss in the Heat's history. Miami only trailed 23–21 after one quarter, but the Hornets clobbered the Heat 58–37 in the second and third quarters. A 20–2 spurt by the Hornets in the third quarter put the game out of reach and the Heat were routed, 106–80.

➲ "Out-Everythinged"

Game 2 was another 26-point drubbing. This time the final score was 102–76. Charlotte completed the sweep on their home court with a convincing 94–79 win. In three games, the Heat averaged a lowly 78.3 points a game while giving up an average of 100.7.

After being swept, Riley freely admitted that Charlotte dominated the Heat in every possible way. "It was no contest," Riley said. "It's a feeling of being outplayed, outcoached, out-every-thinged."[1]

Prior to Game 3, there had been rumors that Riley would announce his retirement. He stopped short of doing that, but he freely acknowledged that he may have reached the lowest point of his pro coaching career. He could not explain why the Heat played so poorly.

"I'm like a basketball coachaholic who's bottomed out," Riley said. "I need to do some deep searching to find out how to coach the Miami Heat."[2]

Very Tough Year

At the start of the 2001–02 season, it looked like Riley still did not have any answers. The Heat got off to their worst start since their horrible 0–17 beginning during the franchise's first season. They lost fourteen of their first sixteen games. That practically ensured that they would not make the playoffs. The terrible start also hurt attendance. In 2000–01, the Heat had sold out twenty home dates at AmericanAirlines Arena. In 2001–02, it was down to twelve.

The Heat finished almost as badly as they started. They lost seven of their last eleven games for a 36–46 record. Miami finished next to last in the Atlantic Division that they used to dominate. Heat fans were no longer regarding Pat Riley as a coaching wizard who would bring the team an NBA title. After leading the team for seven seasons, there was a lot of talk that the game had passed him by.

Riley's Worst Year

The 2002–03 season did not do anything to silence Riley's critics. A dismal 1–7 start and a

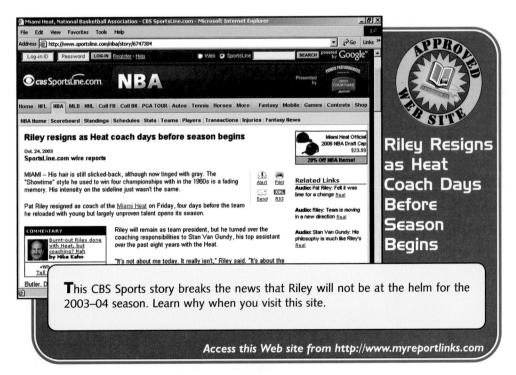

This CBS Sports story breaks the news that Riley will not be at the helm for the 2003–04 season. Learn why when you visit this site.

Access this Web site from http://www.myreportlinks.com

25–57 season kept the fans away in droves. It was Riley's worst record in twenty-one years as an NBA head coach. The Heat only sold out ten of their forty-one home games. For the fourth year in a row, the Heat's average attendance at AmericanAirlines Arena showed a decline.

"If you're not winning, the people are going to stay home," Riley said. "There's other things to do. L.A., New York, Miami, there's other things to do. And if you're winning, people want to be a part of it."[3]

In his last two years as Heat coach, Riley had a record of 61–103. Heat fans were quick to point out that the 61 wins in two years matched their win total for the 1996–97 season. Riley was fifty-eight years old, and many people assumed that he was through as a head coach.

In the off-season, Riley worked hard to revamp the slumping team. He chose Dwyane Wade as their first-round draft pick and signed Udonis Haslem, Lamar Odom, Rafer Alston, Samaki Walker, John Wallace, and Loren Woods as free agents. Then, Riley tossed in one more component to complete the makeover. Four days before the start of the season, he abruptly resigned as the Heat's head coach.

Stan Van Gundy Takes the Reins

At a hastily called news conference on October 24, 2003, Riley explained why he was turning over his

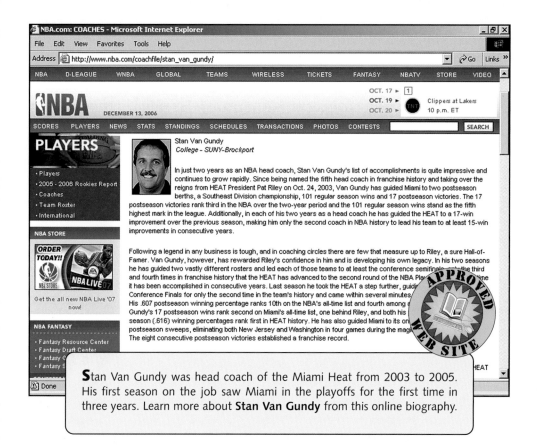

Stan Van Gundy was head coach of the Miami Heat from 2003 to 2005. His first season on the job saw Miami in the playoffs for the first time in three years. Learn more about **Stan Van Gundy** from this online biography.

coaching duties to his longtime assistant coach, Stan Van Gundy.

"I just believe that with this new team and these guys and the flexibility that we have that another voice is needed on the court," Riley said. "I'm firmly convinced about that. And I think that it's Stan's voice. That's why I did this."[4]

Van Gundy was a familiar face to the Heat players and fans. He had been an assistant coach since Riley joined the Heat. Prior to that, he was a college coach for eight years. His brother, Jeff, had been head coach of the New York Knicks during the Heat-Knicks rivalry. Van Gundy was well aware that he was replacing one of the most honored and acclaimed coaches in NBA history. He quickly tried to avoid being compared to Riley. "I'm not going to try to be Pat Riley," Van Gundy insisted. "I'm not looking to make a lot of Pat Riley comparisons."[5]

Riley did not express any regrets about stepping down. He said that he was content to focus on his duties as the Heat's president. "I've been looking forward to the day that I could run an organization without the pressures of having to coach too," Riley said.[6]

Under their new coach, the Heat got off to a very bad start in 2003–04. They lost their first seven games and attendance at home games continued to drop. To make AmericanAirlines Arena look fuller, Heat management began covering the highest level seats with thick black curtains.

Playoff Turnaround

The Heat fell to 5–15 before winning three in a row. At the start of March, they were 25–36 and well on their way to a third straight losing season. But a late-season surge got them into the playoffs. By winning seventeen of their last twenty-one games, Miami finished with a 42–40 record.

Rookies Dwyane Wade and Udonis Haslem helped to spark the turnaround. Wade was named

▲ *Dwyane Wade scans the floor as he drives the Heat offense.*
Wade joined the Heat as a rookie in the 2004–05 season.

to the NBA's All-Rookie First Team and Haslem earned a spot on the All-Rookie Second Team. Eddie Jones, who was the only returning starter from the 2002–03 team, was one the Heat's most consistent players. He led the team in games started (81), scoring (17.3), and free throw percentage (.835).

For the opening round of the playoffs, the Heat faced the 41–41 New Orleans Hornets. The Hornets looked like they would face an early exit after the Heat won the first two games before sellout crowds on their home court. Game 2 was a 93–63 blowout with all five starters scoring in double figures.

A Series Win

After returning to New Orleans, the resilient Hornets evened the series 2–2. In Game 5 in Miami, it looked like the Heat might go down 3–2, when the Hornets led 63–58 after three quarters. A three-point shot by Wade with 54.4 seconds left broke an 80–80 deadlock, and Miami went on to win 87–83. Game 6 continued the trend of the home team winning when a sellout crowd at the New Orleans Arena cheered the Hornets on to an 89–83 win.

A 23-point, 9-rebound performance by Heat forward Caron Butler in Game 7 helped decide the series. After opening up a 71–55 lead with 8:38 left, the Heat held on for an 85–77 win. They

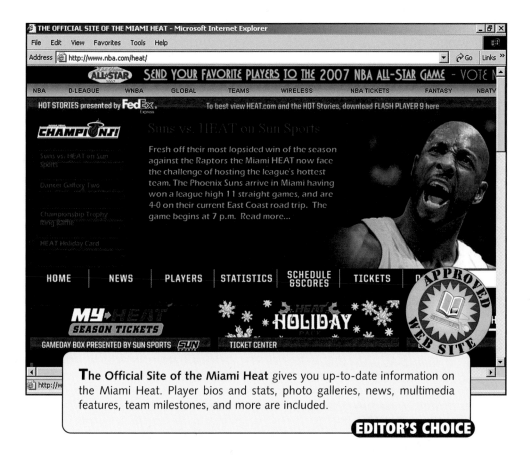

The Official Site of the Miami Heat gives you up-to-date information on the Miami Heat. Player bios and stats, photo galleries, news, multimedia features, team milestones, and more are included.

EDITOR'S CHOICE

advanced to face the Indiana Pacers in the Eastern Conference Semifinals.

Second-Round Showdown

The Pacers had won the Central Division with a record of 61–21. In the first round of the playoffs, they swept the Boston Celtics four games to none. In the regular season, they had played the Heat three times and won all three games.

The first two games were in Indianapolis. The Pacers performed well in front of friendly sold out crowds. In Game 1, Indiana's Ron Artest led all scorers with 25 points, and the Pacers won easily 94–81. Game 2 saw Artest once again leading the Pacers in scoring with 20 points in a 91–80 Pacer victory.

Returning to Miami helped the Heat even up the series. In Game 3, Dwyane Wade scored 25 points, and Heat center Brian Grant grabbed 16 rebounds to lead Miami to a 94–87 win. Wade also dished out 6 assists and made 11 of 12 free throws. Some balanced scoring helped the Heat win Game 4. Lamar Odom (22 points),

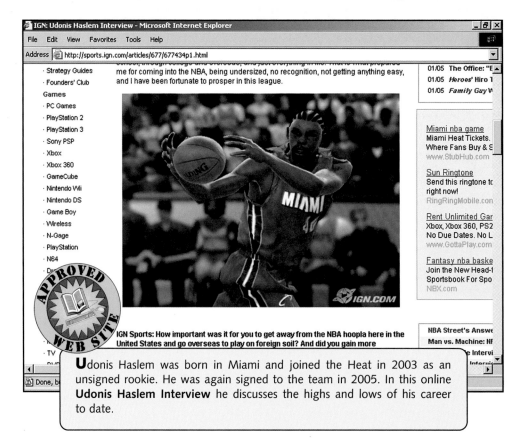

Udonis Haslem was born in Miami and joined the Heat in 2003 as an unsigned rookie. He was again signed to the team in 2005. In this online **Udonis Haslem Interview** he discusses the highs and lows of his career to date.

Caron Butler (21 points), and Wade (20 points) combined to lead the Heat to a 100–88 victory.

Game 5 found the Pacers back on their home court. Pacers center Jeff Foster helped to hold off the Heat with a double-double, scoring 20 points and fetching 16 rebounds. The Pacers opened things up in the second and third quarters by outscoring the Heat 54–34. Six Miami Heat players scored in double figures, but it was not enough to stop the Pacers from winning 94–83.

⊜Hard-Fought Contest

Game 6 gave the Heat a chance to stop the Pacers before a sellout crowd of 20,136 at AmericanAirlines Arena. The Heat had reason to feel good about their chances of winning. They had won their last eighteen home games.

Neither team played very well. The Pacers had 18 turnovers and only made 22 of 68 shots for a sub-par 32.4 shooting percentage. Unfortunately, the Heat's shooting was even worse. Miami only made 25 of 82 shots for 30.5 percent. Both teams shot a lot of three-pointers and missed almost all of them. The Pacers were three of fifteen from beyond the arc, while Miami was one of twelve.

Miami was able to hold the Pacers' all-star forward Jermaine O'Neal to only 7 points after O'Neal had scored 88 points in his last three playoff games. But the difference in the game

A mountain of a man, when Shaquille O'Neal goes up for a dunk most defenders wisely get out of his way.

was rebounding. Indiana had 53 rebounds to Miami's 42. The final result was a 73–70 win for the Pacers.

Most Heat fans would consider the 2003–04 season to have been a successful one. After starting the season 0–7, they turned it around late in the campaign. The Heat won 17 of their final 21 games and advanced to the second round of the playoffs. Two new players—Udonis Haslem and Dwyane Wade—joined with Eddie Jones to form the nucleus of a future championship club.

That championship, though, would not come for two more years. It would take the return of Riley as their coach and the addition of Shaquille O'Neal as their center to get it done.

Pat Riley (left) stands with Heat owner Micky Arison (center) and former head coach Stan Van Gundy (right).

FRONT OFFICE FIRESTARTERS

5

Among the three original owners of the Miami Heat, Billy Cunningham was the member of the trio with the strongest ties to basketball. When he was five years old, Cunningham got a basketball for his birthday. As soon as he gripped the ball, basketball gripped him.

"I couldn't put my finger on it exactly, but there was just something about the game," Cunningham said. "I loved it instantly."[1]

⮕ The Kangaroo Kid

From that day on, basketball was the focus of Cunningham's life. He went on to become a star player in high school, college, and the pros. From 1965 to 1976, Cunningham, known as the Kangaroo Kid for his leaping ability, starred in both the ABA and NBA, earning numerous honors and awards. He played in five All-Star Games and won the ABA's Most Valuable Player Award in 1973. A severe knee injury forced him to retire when he was only thirty-two. "In a way the injury made things easy for me," Cunningham said. "I never had to agonize over that decision (to retire) all athletes face."[2]

In November 1977, Cunningham began his second career in pro basketball as an NBA head coach. He coached the Philadelphia 76ers for eight seasons, compiling a record of 454–196 for a winning percentage of .698. While coaching the 76ers, they went to the NBA Finals three times and won the championship in 1983.

Bufman Gets Cunningham Involved

After leaving coaching, Cunningham became an analyst and broadcaster of NBA games for CBS. An unexpected phone call from Zev Bufman got Cunningham involved in the creation of the Miami Heat. Bufman had been trying to land an NBA franchise for Miami. He needed a well-known basketball figure with experience in the fine points of the game. By that time, Cunningham was a member of the Basketball Hall of Fame. He had been inducted for his considerable playing achievements in 1986.

Cunningham teamed up with Bufman. A short time later, they brought in Cunningham's friend, Lewis Schaffel, as their general manager, and Ted

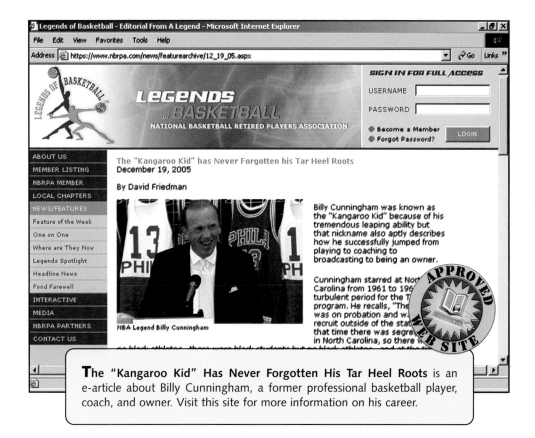

The "Kangaroo Kid" has Never Forgotten his Tar Heel Roots
December 19, 2005

By David Friedman

NBA Legend Billy Cunningham

Billy Cunningham was known as the "Kangaroo Kid" because of his tremendous leaping ability but that nickname also aptly describes how he successfully jumped from playing to coaching to broadcasting to being an owner.

Cunningham starred at North Carolina from 1961 to 196_ turbulent period for the T__ program. He recalls, "The __ was on probation and w__ recruit outside of the stat__ that time there was segre__ in North Carolina, so there __

The "Kangaroo Kid" Has Never Forgotten His Tar Heel Roots is an e-article about Billy Cunningham, a former professional basketball player, coach, and owner. Visit this site for more information on his career.

Arison as a part owner. In 1987, the NBA Board of Governors awarded that group a franchise to begin play in the 1988–89 season.

In 1991–92, the Heat made the playoffs for the first time. That was only their fourth season. Cunningham helped bring about their rapid rise to postseason play with his shrewd use of draft picks and trades.

⊜ Stepping Down

Cunningham ended his association with the Heat in 1995 by selling his share of the franchise to Ted

Arison's son, Micky. One year later, he was honored by being named to the NBA's 50th Anniversary All-Time Team as one of the fifty greatest players in NBA history.

Pat Williams, Senior Executive Vice-President of the Orlando Magic, worked with Cunningham in Philadelphia. He summed up Cunningham's life in basketball by saying:

> When you think about Billy's life, it's amazing. He was a high school superstar. Then he went to North Carolina and was an All-American. He was No. 1 draft choice. Then an all-star. Then he goes into coaching and percentage-wise becomes one of the best ever. He rises to the highest level of broadcasting. Then he enters into the [NBA] expansion pursuit and gets it. It's unbelievable. I don't know anything he's done that hasn't worked. It's a remarkable life.[3]

⬀ Micky Arison

Although his official title is managing general partner, Micky Arison is usually called the Heat's owner. But overseeing one of the NBA's most successful franchises is just another thing that Arison does very well. Since 1990, he has also served as chairman and chief executive officer of the well known cruise ship company, the Carnival Corporation. Since October 2005, Arison has also served as chairman of the NBA Board of Governors.

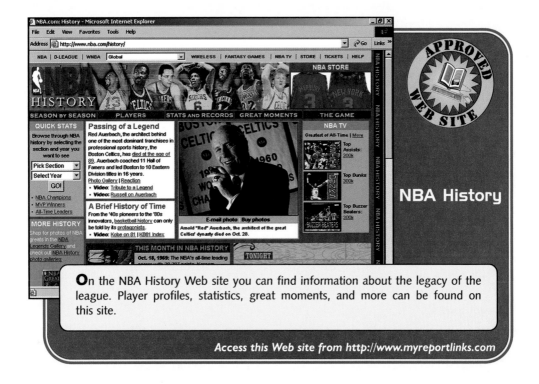

On the NBA History Web site you can find information about the legacy of the league. Player profiles, statistics, great moments, and more can be found on this site.

Access this Web site from http://www.myreportlinks.com

While with the Heat, Arison has shown a strong commitment to improving both the franchise and the quality of life in Miami-Dade County. Arison worked with local government officials to construct the Heat's home court, the state-of-the-art AmericanAirlines Arena. The building allowed the Heat to keep its corporate offices in downtown Miami. Arison has also supported many community service organizations including the United Way and Community Partnership for the Homeless.

Heat coach and president Pat Riley credits Arison with doing everything he could to bring the

Heat their first NBA championship in 2006. "Micky's been a great owner," Riley said. "He's been very good to me, and I think that he's been a great owner from the standpoint of being able to provide for me everything that we need to try to be successful."[4]

Zev Bufman

Along with Ted Arison and Billy Cunningham, Zev Bufman worked to bring the NBA to Miami and make the Heat a successful franchise. Although he's no longer associated with the Heat, Bufman

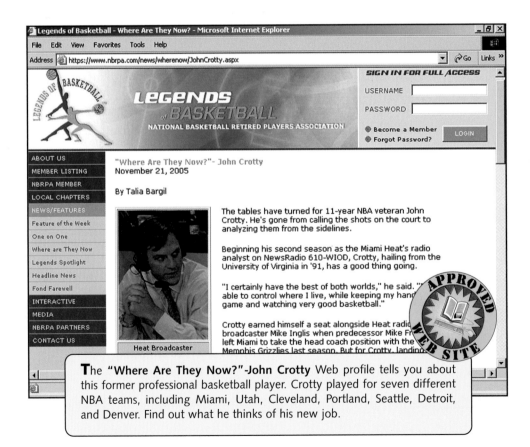

The "Where Are They Now?"-John Crotty Web profile tells you about this former professional basketball player. Crotty played for seven different NBA teams, including Miami, Utah, Cleveland, Portland, Seattle, Detroit, and Denver. Find out what he thinks of his new job.

is remembered for being one of the movers and shakers that brought pro basketball to Miami. Bufman also worked to arrange the financing for the AmericanAirlines Arena where the Heat, currently play.

As a producer of Broadway plays, Bufman had years of experience in fundraising. By showing the NBA that Miami could, and would, support an expansion team, Bufman laid the foundation for a successful franchise.

Eric Reid

Another person who has been with the Heat from the start of the franchise is their television play-by-play announcer, Eric Reid. Reid began working for the Heat as a TV/radio color analyst. During the Heat's fourth season (1991–92), Reid began doing the play-by-play. His familiar voice has been a part of over 1,300 regular season broadcasts of Heat games.

Mike Inglis and Jose Paneda

For fans following the Heat on radio, Mike Inglis handles the English language broadcasts and Jose Paneda is the voice of their Spanish broadcasts. Before joining the Heat, Inglis worked as the radio voice of the Indiana Pacers, and then the Toronto Raptors. Paneda has been with the Heat since their inception. In 2002, Paneda became the first

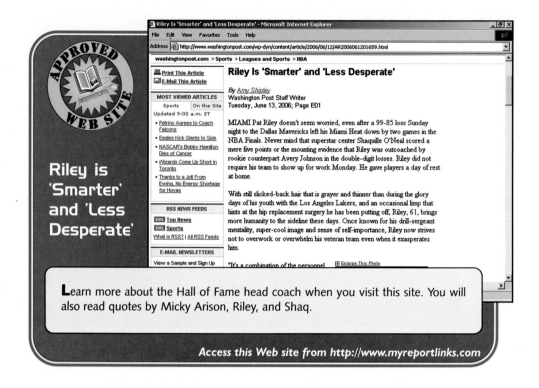

Riley is 'Smarter' and 'Less Desperate'

Riley Is 'Smarter' and 'Less Desperate'

By *Amy Shipley*
Washington Post Staff Writer
Tuesday, June 13, 2006; Page E01

MIAMI Pat Riley doesn't seem worried, even after a 99-85 loss Sunday night to the Dallas Mavericks left his Miami Heat down by two games in the NBA Finals. Never mind that superstar center Shaquille O'Neal scored a mere five points or the mounting evidence that Riley was outcoached by rookie counterpart Avery Johnson in the double-digit losses. Riley did not require his team to show up for work Monday. He gave players a day of rest at home.

With still slicked-back hair that is grayer and thinner than during the glory days of his youth with the Los Angeles Lakers, and an occasional limp that hints at the hip replacement surgery he has been putting off, Riley, 61, brings more humanity to the sideline these days. Once known for his drill-sergeant mentality, super-cool image and sense of self-importance, Riley now strives not to overwork or overwhelm his veteran team even when it exasperates him.

"It's a combination of the personnel

Learn more about the Hall of Fame head coach when you visit this site. You will also read quotes by Micky Arison, Riley, and Shaq.

Access this Web site from http://www.myreportlinks.com

Heat broadcaster to announce one thousand consecutive regular season games.

Pat Riley

The one person most closely associated with the Heat's recent success is their coach and team president, Pat Riley. His brilliant trade for Shaquille O'Neal and the drafting of Dwyane Wade will be long remembered as the moves that brought the Heat a championship.

Along with winning five NBA championships, Riley is also an outstanding motivational speaker. His shrewd evaluations of basketball talent and his ability to assemble championship teams bode well for his eventual election to the Naismith Memorial Basketball Hall of Fame.

In every pro sports franchise there is a team behind the team. It is a collection of coaches, scouts, owners, trainers, and broadcasters. Under Riley and company, the Heat have assembled one of the best.

Extremely loyal to their team, Miami Heat fans turned out to the AmericanAirlines Arena to cheer them on for Game 6 of the 2006 NBA Finals even though the game was being played in Dallas.

THE NBA LIFE 6

It has been said that when professional athletes work they play, and when they play they work. There are plenty of times when the game is fun, like when they are blowing out an opponent and coasting to an easy victory. NBA players ride in chartered jets, stay in the best hotels, and get a generous stipend for eating at the best restaurants. Still, they also lead a very structured life once the season begins. Before, between, and after games, there are many demands on their time.

For a team advancing to the championship round of the playoffs, the NBA season lasts over seven-and-half months. When you add in the preseason training camps and exhibition games, an NBA player on a championship team is on the job from early October to late June.

The Preseason

Preseason training camp starts in early October. All the players under contract, plus a few free agent invitees, convene to scrimmage and vie for the thirteen to fifteen spots on the team's roster. Under league rules, an NBA team must have twelve active players plus a minimum of one and a maximum of three inactive players on their roster. It is not unusual for an NBA team to have ten to twelve core players already assured of a spot on the roster when the preseason camp begins.

Unless the player is a veteran star signed to a multiyear contract, there is an intense pressure to perform well and impress the coaches. The cuts come quickly, since the first exhibition games usually begin during the second week of October.

Most of the time, a team plays six to eight exhibition games before the final cuts are made. The brief exhibition season gives the coaching staff an opportunity to see how inexperienced rookies and other new players will perform in game situations. For a marginal player, a poor exhibition season can mean the end of his dream of playing in the NBA.

An impressive exhibition season will enhance, but not ensure a player's chances of being on the team's opening-day roster. Sometimes, a player cut from one team will get signed by another team

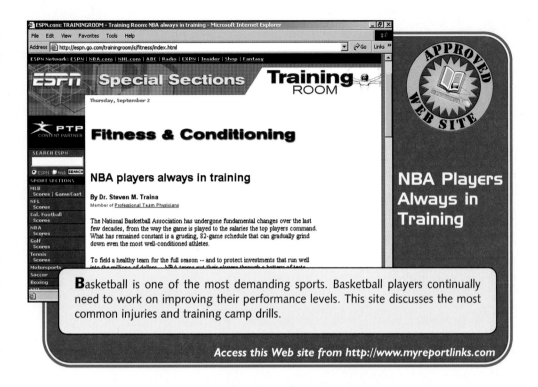

ESPN.com: TRAININGROOM - Training Room: NBA always in training - Microsoft Internet Explorer

File   Edit   View   Favorites   Tools   Help

Address http://espn.go.com/trainingroom/s/fitness/index.html   Go   Links

ESPN Network: ESPN | NBA.com | NHL.com | ABC | Radio | EXPN | Insider | Shop | Fantasy

ESPN   Special Sections   Training ROOM

Thursday, September 2

Fitness & Conditioning

NBA players always in training

By Dr. Steven M. Traina
Member of Professional Team Physicians

The National Basketball Association has undergone fundamental changes over the last few decades, from the way the game is played to the salaries the top players command. What has remained constant is a grueling, 82-game schedule that can gradually grind down even the most well-conditioned athletes.

To field a healthy team for the full season -- and to protect investments that run well into the millions of dollars -- NBA teams put their players through a battery of tests

NBA Players Always in Training

Basketball is one of the most demanding sports. Basketball players continually need to work on improving their performance levels. This site discusses the most common injuries and training camp drills.

Access this Web site from http://www.myreportlinks.com

before opening day. That generally happens when he has both a good agent and a good preseason.

Starting the Season

After the rosters are finalized, the team settles into playing three to four games a week. But, there are times that a team will play as many as four games in five days. The amount of time an NBA team spends in practice and preparation varies with what the schedule allows and how many games they have already played. As the season moves along, the time for practice and preparation diminishes. Players come to instinctively know what to do and what to expect from their teammates.

Gloria Pombo (right) enthusiastically paints the face of fellow fan Grace Salazar before the Heat's contest on June 20, 2006.

Shortly after a game, an NBA team on a road trip will board a chartered jet to take it to the next city. Typically, they will arrive at their hotel between 1:00 and 3:00 A.M. The players check into their rooms, unwind, and try to get some sleep. Some may call room service for a late night snack before dozing off. Then, the team will meet around eleven o'clock in the morning for a late breakfast and a viewing of a videotape of the previous night's game. After breakfast, a bus takes them to the arena for a short practice session.

Game Day

Most of the time, the home team gets the court first for a game-day practice. They will use the court for around an hour before the visiting team is allowed on the floor. During the overlapping time when one team is leaving and the other is arriving, the opposing players may briefly socialize. It is not uncommon for opposing players to be former teammates from college or other NBA teams. They may even make plans for some more socializing after the game.

The socializing is often cut short by the shrill sound of a coach blowing a whistle. The players snap to it and commence their workout. Unless the team has been performing poorly, the visitor's practice is also around an hour. The players will loosen up with some pregame shooting known as a shootaround. The shootaround has become a standard practice for every NBA team. It lasts about sixty minutes and lets the players loosen up and concentrate on perfecting their shooting touch. After the shootaround, the head coach and his staff will go over a scouting report and show a video of their opponent. This also gives the team trainer time to tend to any injuries or nagging aches and pains that are bothering the players.

During their free time on the road, most players rest and relax by playing cards or video games. Others will watch television or DVDs or take a nap. Around 5:30 P.M. the early bus takes the rookies and the reserve players to the arena. They are the first to leave so they can get in some extra practice time. Around six o'clock in the evening, a second bus takes the veteran players and starters to the arena.

⊜ Off Days

When the team has a day off between games, the coach holds just a morning practice. The team practices against plays they expect its opponent to use. The players review defensive matchups and also review the tendencies, strengths, and weaknesses of their opponent's individual players. They will also review and practice offensive plays that

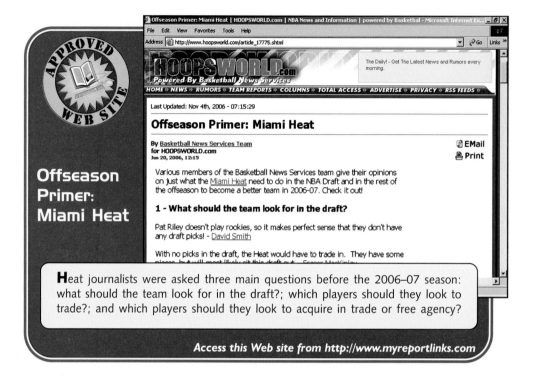

Offseason
Primer:
Miami Heat

Offseason Primer: Miami Heat | HOOPSWORLD.com | NBA News and Information | powered by Basketbal - Microsoft Internet Ex...

File   Edit   View   Favorites   Tools   Help

Address http://www.hoopsworld.com/article_17775.shtml   Go   Links »

HOOPSWORLD.com
Powered By Basketball News Services

The Daily! - Get The Latest News and Rumors every morning.

HOME » NEWS » RUMORS » TEAM REPORTS » COLUMNS » TOTAL ACCESS » ADVERTISE » PRIVACY » RSS FEEDS »

Last Updated: Nov 4th, 2006 - 07:15:29

Offseason Primer: Miami Heat

By Basketball News Services Team
for HOOPSWORLD.com   EMail
Jun 20, 2006, 12:15   Print

Various members of the Basketball News Services team give their opinions on just what the Miami Heat need to do in the NBA Draft and in the rest of the offseason to become a better team in 2006-07. Check it out!

1 - What should the team look for in the draft?

Pat Riley doesn't play rookies, so it makes perfect sense that they don't have any draft picks! - David Smith

With no picks in the draft, the Heat would have to trade in. They have some

Heat journalists were asked three main questions before the 2006–07 season: what should the team look for in the draft?; which players should they look to trade?; and which players should they look to acquire in trade or free agency?

Access this Web site from http://www.myreportlinks.com

they think will be effective against their next opponent.

Most players enjoy a sizable lunch after a morning practice. The preferred dishes are pasta, salads, and fish instead of fried or fatty foods. If they are not on the road, they often spend the afternoon hours with their families and friends or conferring with their business associates. At other times, the players are obliged to make personal appearances at team-sponsored events like visiting schools or the children's wing of a hospital.

During a home stand, players enjoy a bit more free time and it is less stressful knowing that they will be playing in front of a friendly crowd.

Practice sessions are held to get the players mentally, physically, and emotionally ready for the game. Whether it is the first preseason exhibition game or Game 7 of the championship finals, the best prepared team is the team most likely to win.

▲ Shaquille O'Neal muscles in on Pistons center Ben Wallace as he looks to get an inside shot. Shaq is widely considered to be one of the best players in basketball history.

MIAMI HEAT STARS

7

Although the Heat is one of the NBA's younger franchises, it has had some truly outstanding players during its eighteen seasons in the league. At different times, Heat players have won NBA awards for Player of the Week, Player of the Month, Defensive Player of the Year, Most Improved Player, and have been selected to All-NBA First and Second Teams. Heat players have also been named to the NBA's All-Rookie and All-Defensive teams.

→ Shaq

Shaquille O'Neal has only played a few seasons for the Heat, but many NBA watchers and Heat fans regard him as the greatest player in team history. When he began playing for the Orlando Magic in 1992, O'Neal made an immediate impact on the NBA.

Shaq became the first player to be named Player of the Week during his first week in the NBA. Before being named Rookie of the Year, Shaq was the league's Rookie of the Month for four months during the regular season. The season before Shaq joined the Magic they were 21–61. In his rookie season, they improved to 41–41.

During his fifth season in the NBA, Shaq was named to the league's 50th Anniversary All-Time Team. At the age of twenty-four, the dominating seven-foot one-inch center was already considered one of the fifty greatest players in NBA history. He was the youngest player to receive that honor. Before joining the Heat, Shaq played on three consecutive NBA championship teams with the Lakers (2000–02) and was voted the NBA Finals MVP three years in a row.

Going to Miami

In July 2004, the Heat acquired O'Neal from the Lakers in exchange for three players and a future first-round draft pick. When the Heat announced the acquisition of the superstar center, team president Pat Riley said: "Today the Miami Heat took a giant step forward in our continued pursuit of an NBA championship. "We feel that we have traded for the best player in the NBA."[1]

Age and injuries have somewhat reduced Shaq's playing time since he joined the Heat. Still, he has averaged 21.6 points and 9.9 rebounds a game while playing around 32 minutes a contest for them.

⊜Dwyane Wade

Along with Shaquille O'Neal, six-foot four-inch shooting guard Dwyane Wade has been a major factor in the Heat's recent rise to become one of the NBA's elite teams. Wade was Miami's first pick in the 2003 NBA draft and was the fifth player chosen overall. In Wade's rookie season, the Heat improved from 27–57 to 42–40. His first-year stats of 16.2 points, 4.5 assists, and 4.0 rebounds per game made him a unanimous choice for the NBA's All-Rookie First Team.

As he has matured as a player, Wade's stats have steadily improved. After three seasons, he has averaged 22.9 points and 1.9 steals per game along with grabbing over 5.0 rebounds and dishing out over 6.0 assists per game. At the age of twenty-four, Wade is already a two-time all-star.

Wade credits his year of ineligibility at Marquette University with helping to mold him into becoming an outstanding all-around player. When he was stuck on the practice squad, he learned to play every position.

"I played the role of the upcoming opponent's star in every practice," Wade recalled. "One day I

Dwyane Wade hits a fall-away jumper over Adrian Griffin of the Dallas Mavericks. Wade is one of the most exciting young players in the NBA.

had to be a point guard, the next a post player, the next a 3-point shooter."[2]

Rony Seikaly

Rony Seikaly was the first player drafted by the Miami Heat and he ably performed at center for the team's first six seasons. Although he was not a dominating player, Seikaly was a very dependable scorer and rebounder. For five consecutive seasons (1989–90 to 1993–94), Seikaly averaged double figures in both scoring and rebounding. He still holds the Heat team record for most rebounds in a game (34).

Seikaly's breakthrough season came in 1990 when he averaged 16.6 points and 10.4 rebounds per game for Miami to win the NBA's Most Improved Player Award. After the 1994 season, the Heat traded Seikaly to the Golden State Warriors. Seikaly continued to play in the NBA until 1999. When he retired, he had career averages of 14.7 points and 9.5 rebounds per game.

Alonzo Mourning

Two seasons after the Heat traded Seikaly, Alonzo Mourning became Miami's starting center. During his tenure with the Heat, "Zo" (as he is called) has been selected to the league's All-Defensive and All-NBA first teams. In 1999 and 2000, Mourning won back-to-back NBA Defensive Player of the

Alonzo Mourning drives to the basket against Zaza Pachulia of the Atlanta Hawks. Mourning came back in 2004 for his second stint with the Heat.

Year Awards. During those two seasons, Mourning also led the NBA in blocked shots and blocked shots per game.

Mourning explained that the key to playing good defense was to focus on your man and do not try to do too much.

"I keep my body between the man, the ball and the basket, " Mourning said. "I can't stop everybody. I try to contain my opponent and make him take difficult shots."[3]

A Valiant Return

A recent comeback from a potentially fatal disease may be Mourning's most remarkable accomplishment. After being diagnosed with a serious kidney disorder Mourning refused to retire. He loved the game too much to give it up. When doctors told him that the disease was life threatening if he kept playing, Mourning reluctantly retired in November 2003.

About a month later, Mourning received a kidney transplant from his cousin, Jason Cooper. Ten months after the operation, Mourning was playing again. In March 2005, the Heat signed Mourning as a free agent. Since then the six-foot ten-inch center has served the team as a capable backup for Shaquille O'Neal.

A seven-time All-Star, Mourning is currently the Heat's all-time leader in field goal percentage,

▲ Glen Rice is one of the greatest scorers in team history. He is among the all-time NBA leaders in three-point shooting.

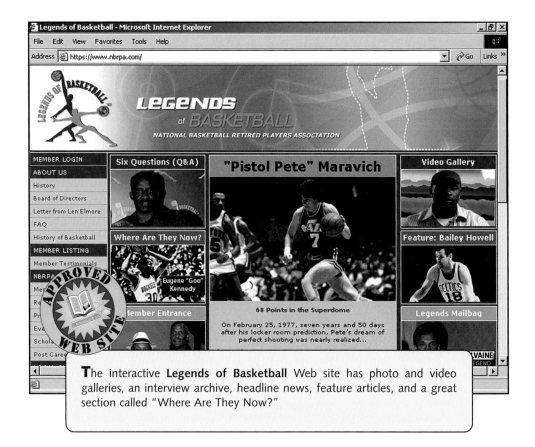

LEGENDS
of BASKETBALL
NATIONAL BASKETBALL RETIRED PLAYERS ASSOCIATION

MEMBER LOGIN
ABOUT US
History
Board of Directors
Letter from Len Elmore
FAQ
History of Basketball
MEMBER LISTING
Member Testimonials
NBRPA
Me
Re
Pr
Ev
Schol
Post Care

Six Questions (Q&A)

Where Are They Now?

Eugene "Goo" Kennedy

Member Entrance

"Pistol Pete" Maravich

68 Points in the Superdome

On February 25, 1977, seven years and 50 days after his locker room prediction, Pete's dream of perfect shooting was nearly realized...

Video Gallery

Feature: Bailey Howell

Legends Mailbag

The interactive **Legends of Basketball** Web site has photo and video galleries, an interview archive, headline news, feature articles, and a great section called "Where Are They Now?"

blocked shots, free throw attempts, and free throws made.

⊖ Glen Rice

Glen Rice joined the Heat in 1989 after they made the six-foot eight-inch forward their first draft choice. Rice had led the University of Michigan to an NCAA championship before turning professional. He quickly became one of the Heat's most consistent players in the early days of the franchise.

While playing for the Heat from 1989 to 1995, Rice averaged 19.3 points and 4.9 rebounds a game. A soft shooting touch and superior leaping ability allowed Rice to score from both beyond the arc and in the paint. Rice holds the Miami team records for most career points (9,248) and most points in a game (56).

Recalling his team record 56-point performance against the Orlando Magic, Rice said, "There are certain times when a shooter feels like even the longest shots are layups. As you lift and release, it's like the rim has expanded to three feet wide. I was feeling that for this entire game."[4]

If a defender thought that he could keep Rice from scoring by fouling him, he would usually end up getting burned. Rice's free throw percentage of .835 makes him the most accurate foul shooter to play for the Heat.

Along with being a scoring threat, Rice was both a very durable player and a tough defender. He is the Heat's all-time leader in consecutive games played (174) and minutes played (17,059). Rice also led the Heat in steals for two consecutive seasons. In November 1995, the Heat traded Rice to the Charlotte Hornets in a deal that brought Alonzo Mourning to Miami.

Tim Hardaway

From 1996 to 2001, Tim Hardaway averaged 17.4 points and 7.8 assists as the Heat's point guard. Hardaway was originally drafted by the

Tim Hardaway slices through Patrick Ewing and Charlie Ward for an easy lay-up in this 1997 game against the New York Knicks. Hardaway was famous for his nearly unstoppable crossover dribble.

Golden State Warriors in the first round of the 1989 NBA draft. Although he was barely six feet tall, Hardaway quickly showed that he could play with the league's biggest and tallest stars. He was a unanimous choice for the NBA's All-Rookie Team.

After Miami acquired him, Hardaway teamed up with Alonzo Mourning to bolster the team both offensively and defensively. Offensively, he utilized a devastating crossover dribble to drive to the hoop at full speed. When opposing defenders backed away from him, Hardaway would stop behind the arc and swish in a three-point shot. Defensively, he would easily move into the passing lanes to pick off passes that went awry.

While playing for the Heat, Hardaway led the team in assists for five consecutive seasons and in steals for three years in a row. He also represented the Heat in two All-Star Games. Still, he is best remembered for a crossover dribble that left opponents shaking their heads. Hall-of-Fame player Magic Johnson described Hardaway's crossover move by saying: "It can't be stopped. It's bang, bang, and you're dead."[5]

Jamal Mashburn

Although he only played for the Heat for four seasons, six-foot eight-inch forward Jamal Mashburn

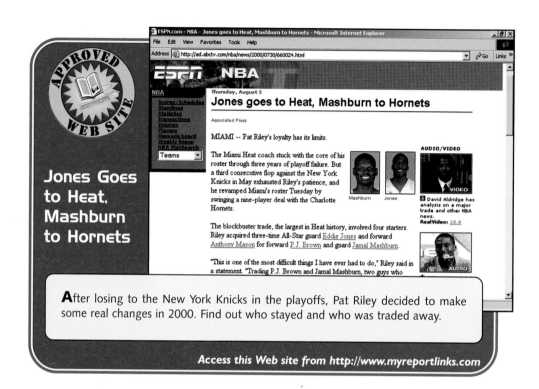

ESPN NBA

NBA
Scores/Schedules
Standings
Statistics
Transactions
Injuries
Players
Message board
Weekly lineup
NBA StatSearch

Teams

Thursday, August 3
Jones goes to Heat, Mashburn to Hornets

Associated Press

MIAMI -- Pat Riley's loyalty has its limits.

The Miami Heat coach stuck with the core of his roster through three years of playoff failure. But a third consecutive flop against the New York Knicks in May exhausted Riley's patience, and he revamped Miami's roster Tuesday by swinging a nine-player deal with the Charlotte Hornets.

Mashburn   Jones

The blockbuster trade, the largest in Heat history, involved four starters. Riley acquired three-time All-Star guard Eddie Jones and forward Anthony Mason for forward P.J. Brown and guard Jamal Mashburn.

"This is one of the most difficult things I have ever had to do," Riley said in a statement. "Trading P.J. Brown and Jamal Mashburn, two guys who

AUDIO/VIDEO

VIDEO
David Aldridge has analysis on a major trade and other NBA news.
RealVideo: 28.8

AUDIO

Jones Goes to Heat, Mashburn to Hornets

After losing to the New York Knicks in the playoffs, Pat Riley decided to make some real changes in 2000. Find out who stayed and who was traded away.

Access this Web site from http://www.myreportlinks.com

is fondly remembered by Heat fans as one of their vital players in the late 1990s. After joining the Heat, Mashburn teamed with Miami's established stars Mourning and Hardaway to lead the team to a 61–21 record and an Atlantic Division championship in 1997. With Mashburn's rebounding and defense helping out, the Heat won four consecutive Atlantic Division championships from 1997 to 2000.

During his tenure with the Heat, Mashburn showed his versatility at the small forward position by averaging 15.8 points, 5.2 rebounds, and 3.4 assists per game. In August 2000, the Heat traded Mashburn to the Charlotte Hornets in a major deal involving nine players.

Steve Smith

Although he only played for Miami for four years, six-foot eight-inch guard Steve Smith is remembered for having an immediate effect on the team's improvement. After making Smith their first-round pick in 1991, the Heat improved from 24 wins to 38. Smith was a smooth ball handler, a capable rebounder, and an accurate passer. Smith's rookie season was the first year that the Heat made the playoffs. That year, Smith was also selected to the NBA's All-Rookie First Team.

In his four seasons with the Heat, Smith averaged 15.2 points, 3.9 rebounds, and 5.0 assists per game. Smith left the Heat in November 1994 when they traded him to the Atlanta Hawks.

Grant Long

Grant Long, a six-foot nine-inch power forward, joined the Heat for its inaugural season in 1988–89 and played for them until 1995. At different times in his career, Long led the Heat in games played, starts, minutes played, offensive rebounds, free throws, and steals.

Eddie Jones

For four consecutive seasons (2000–01 to 2003–04), six-foot six-inch guard Eddie Jones

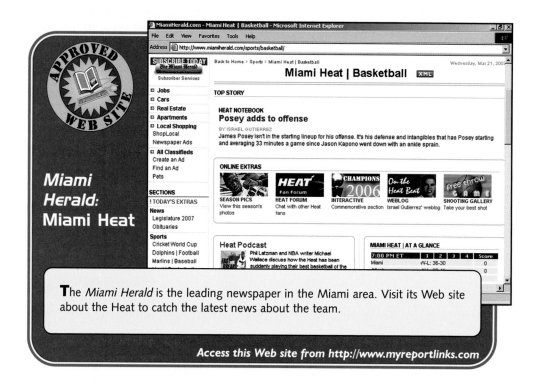

File Edit View Favorites Tools Help

Address http://www.miamiherald.com/sports/basketball/

SUBSCRIBE TODAY
The Miami Herald
Subscriber Services

Back to Home > Sports > Miami Heat | Basketball

Wednesday, Mar 21, 2007

Miami Heat | Basketball XML

□ Jobs
□ Cars
□ Real Estate
□ Apartments
□ Local Shopping
ShopLocal
Newspaper Ads
□ All Classifieds
Create an Ad
Find an Ad
Pets

TOP STORY

HEAT NOTEBOOK
Posey adds to offense

BY ISRAEL GUTIERREZ

James Posey isn't in the starting lineup for his offense. It's his defense and intangibles that has Posey starting and averaging 33 minutes a game since Jason Kapono went down with an ankle sprain.

ONLINE EXTRAS

SECTIONS
! TODAY'S EXTRAS
News
Legislature 2007
Obituaries
Sports
Cricket World Cup
Dolphins | Football
Marlins | Baseball

SEASON PICS
View this season's photos

HEAT FORUM
Fan Forum
Chat with other Heat fans

INTERACTIVE
Commemorative section

WEBLOG
On the Heat Beat
Israel Gutierrez' weblog

SHOOTING GALLERY
Take your best shot

Heat Podcast

Phil Latzman and NBA writer Michael Wallace discuss how the Heat has been suddenly playing their best basketball of the

MIAMI HEAT | AT A GLANCE

7:00 PM ET		1	2	3	4	Score
Miami	W-L: 36-30					0
						0

Miami Herald: Miami Heat

The *Miami Herald* is the leading newspaper in the Miami area. Visit its Web site about the Heat to catch the latest news about the team.

Access this Web site from http://www.myreportlinks.com

was the Heat's leading scorer. During that span, Jones averaged 17.8 points per game, but he also helped the team with his rebounding (4.4 a game) and playmaking (3.2 assists per game). With O'Neal and Wade doing more scoring, Jones became less of a scorer the next two seasons. But it is a role he quickly accepted.

"I was OK with the change because I knew that it was going to make us a better ball club," Jones said. "When you're on a good team, you have to sacrifice some. It wasn't a problem for me to sacrifice offense to help this team win."[6] The Heat traded Jones to the Memphis Grizzlies in August 2005.

⮕ Jon Sundvold

Although he was rarely in the starting lineup, six-foot two-inch guard Jon Sundvold deserves a special mention for a specialized talent. When the Heat needed someone in the lineup as a long range scoring threat, Sundvold would come off the bench. During the Heat's first season, Sundvold sank 48 of 92 shots launched from beyond the arc for an impressive .522 shooting percentage. That was the best three-point shooting percentage in the NBA that season, and John Sundvold became the first Heat player to be a league leader.

Report Links

The Internet sites described below can be accessed at http://www.myreportlinks.com

▶**The Official Site of the Miami Heat**
Editor's Choice Visit this official site for news of the Miami Heat.

▶**NBA.com**
Editor's Choice The official Web site of the National Basketball Association.

▶**Miami Heat Through the Years**
Editor's Choice Browse this *Sports Illustrated* site for Miami Heat photos.

▶**The Official Site of Dwyane Wade**
Editor's Choice Learn about Miami Heat superstar Dwyane Wade.

▶**Shaq Central**
Editor's Choice This site is dedicated to Miami center Shaquille O'Neal.

▶**Pat Riley**
Editor's Choice An online biography of Coach Riley.

▶**Alonzo Mourning**
This player page for Alonzo Mourning has his career stats.

▶**Carnival Founder Ted Arison Dies in Israel**
Learn more about the Miami Heat owner when you visit this Web site.

▶**CNN/SI: "Miami Bounced"**
An article about the crushing loss to the Knicks in the 1999 playoffs.

▶**Heat Coach Van Gundy Resigns; Riley Returns**
This ESPN article discusses the return of Riley.

▶**Jones Goes to Heat, Mashburn to Hornets**
Read about the largest trade in Heat history.

▶**The "Kangaroo Kid" Has Never Forgotten his Tar Heel Roots**
Billy Cunningham was one of the founding co-owners of the Miami Heat.

▶**Legends of Basketball**
This is the official website of the National Basketball Retired Players Association.

▶**Miami Heat**
This site offers complete coverage of the Miami Heat.

▶**Miami Heat Draft History**
Draft information for the Miami Heat can be found on this site.

Report Links

The Internet sites described below can be accessed at http://www.myreportlinks.com

▶Miami Heat Team Page
Visit this *Sports Illustrated* site for information on the Miami Heat.

▶*Miami Herald:* Miami Heat
An online Miami-area newspaper that covers the Heat.

▶Mourning to Sit Out Season
This is the announcement telling fans that Mourning was too sick to play.

▶NBA History
Learn about the history of the National Basketball Association.

▶NBA Players Always in Training
This Web site describes a day in the life of an athlete.

▶The Official Web Site of the Basketball Hall of Fame
The best players in history are enshrined in the Naismith Memorial Basketball Hall of Fame.

▶Offseason Primer: Miami Heat
Read what some sports journalists are saying about the Heat.

▶Riley is 'Smarter' and 'Less Desperate'
This *Washington Post* article provides some interesting insight into Pat Riley.

▶Riley Resigns as Heat Coach Days Before Season Begins
Pat Riley tenders his resignation as head coach of the Heat.

▶Ron Rothstein
Read a short career overview for Ron Rothstein.

▶Stan Van Gundy
This is an overview of Van Gundy's career.

▶Trivia Quiz: Test Your Knowledge of the Heat's Playoff Past
This trivia quiz will teach you a few things about the Heat.

▶Too Hot to Handle! Heat Win First NBA Title
This MSNBC.com article describes a major win for the Heat.

▶Udonis Haslem Interview
Udonis Haslem talks about his coach, career, and how he ended up playing for his hometown.

▶"Where are They Now"—John Crotty
Find out more about Miami Heat's radio analyst from this site.

PLAYER	SEASONS	YRS	G	REB	AST	BLK	STL	PTS	AVG
P. J. Brown	1997–2000	13	999	7,994	1,603	1,056	883	9,395	9.4
Sherman Douglas	1990–92	12	765	1,672	4,536	76	785	8,425	11
Kevin Edwards	1989–93	11	604	1,653	1,609	197	825	6,596	10.9
Tim Hardaway	1996–2001	13	867	2,855	7,095	129	1,428	15,373	17.7
Eddie Jones	2001–05	12	843	3,535	2,634	562	1,526	13,486	16
Grant Long	1989–95	15	1,003	6,154	1,716	366	1,199	9,518	9.5
Jamal Mashburn	1997–2000	11	611	3,271	2,414	109	632	11,644	19.1
Alonzo Mourning	1996–2002 2005–06	13	736	6,694	921	2,136	397	13,501	18.3
Shaquille O'Neal	2005–06	14	941	11,082	2,622	2,377	619	24,764	26.3
Glen Rice	1990–95	15	1,000	4,387	2,097	265	958	18,336	18.3
Rony Seikaly	1989–94	11	678	6,424	860	872	453	9,991	14.7
Steve Smith	1992–95 2005	14	942	3,060	2,922	274	726	13,430	14.3
Jon Sundvold	1989–92	9	502	554	1,469	5	220	3,886	7.7
Dwyane Wade	2004–06	3	213	413	500	67	136	1,881	22.9
Kevin Willis	1995–96	20	1,419	11,893	1,327	749	956	17,241	12.2

Seasons=Seasons with Heat
YRS=Years in NBA
STL=Steals

G=Games Played
REB=Rebounds
PTS=Points Scored

AST=Assists
BLK=Blocks
AVG=Points Per Game

STATS

	HEAD COACHES			
YEAR	COACH	W	L	RESULT
1988–89	Ron Rothstein	15	67	6th place in division
1989–90	Ron Rothstein	18	64	5th place in division
1990–91	Ron Rothstein	24	58	6th place in division
1991–92	Kevin Loughery	38	44	Lost in playoff Rd. 1
1992–93	Kevin Loughery	36	46	5th place in division
1993–94	Kevin Loughery	42	40	Lost in playoff Rd. 1
1994–95	Kevin Loughery	17	29	
	Alvin Gentry	15	21	4th place in division
1995–96	Pat Riley	42	40	Lost in playoff Rd. 1
1996–97	Pat Riley	61	21	Lost in Conference Finals
1997–98	Pat Riley	55	27	Lost in playoff Rd. 1
1998–99	Pat Riley	33	17	Lost in playoff Rd. 1
1999–2000	Pat Riley	52	30	Lost in Conference Semifinals
2000–01	Pat Riley	50	32	Lost in playoff Rd. 1
2001–02	Pat Riley	36	46	6th place in division
2002–03	Pat Riley	25	57	7th place in division
2003–04	Stan Van Gundy	42	40	Lost in Conference Semifinals
2004–05	Stan Van Gundy	59	23	Lost in Conference Finals
2005–06	Stan Van Gundy	11	10	
	Pat Riley	41	20	Won NBA Championship

W=Wins   L=Losses

acquisition—Obtain something by a trade, sale, or other means.

caliber— A level of excellence or importance.

clincher—A victory that secures a win in a series.

consecutive—One after the other without interruption, two or more in a row.

déjà vu—The feeling of previously experiencing a current occurrence.

double-double—When a player makes ten or more of two of the following categories: points, rebounds, assists, or blocks, in one game.

draft—The selection of college and foreign players each year by NBA teams. Normally the teams with the worst records get to choose first.

drubbing—A sound defeat in which one team is not competitive.

exhibition game—Game played that does not count as a victory or loss for either team. The game is usually played during preseason to prepare players for the upcoming season and to determine who will play during the regular season.

flagrant—So obvious that one cannot deny they did not hear or see it.

franchise—A team that has membership in a professional sports league.

free agent—A professional player who is free to negotiate a contract with any team.

intercepted—Interrupted or stopped. In basketball, when a player intercepts a pass made by the opposing team, he catches the ball so that it is now in his team's possession.

mandated—Ordered or required by someone or a group in charge.

revamp—Revitalize and strengthen. Bring life into again.

rookie—A first-year player.

sub-par—Below average.

sweep—A series victory in which one team wins all of the games, without the other team winning even one.

synonymous—Closely associated with.

tenure—Time spent with an organization or in a job.

top-seeded—The top rated team in a playoff or tournament.

trounce—To beat completely. Another word commonly used in the sports world that means the same as trounce is rout.

turnover—Giving up possession of the ball to the opposing team.

unyielding—Not bending, inflexible.

Chapter 1. All Aboard for a Championship

1. "Wade, O'Neal Spark Heat to 2–1 Over Pistons," *2006 Playoffs*, 2006, <http://www.nba.com/games/20060527/DETMIA/recap.html> (January 5, 2007).

2. Jack McCallum, "Miami Exit; Pat Riley quit as Heat coach, but will he return to the bench elsewhere?" *Sports Illustrated*, November 3, 2000, p. 91.

3. Brett Ballantini, "A steal of a deal: with Shaquille O'Neal in tow, Miami's president has set the Heat's sights on one thing: winning an NBA title," *Basketball Digest*, November/December 2004, <http://findarticles.com/p/articles/mi_m0FCJ/is_1_32/ai_n6332441> (December 1, 2006).

4. S. L. Price, "Pat Riley Won't Give In," *Sports Illustrated*, May 1, 2006, p. 64.

5. Chris Ballard, "It Was All In A Night's Work," *Sports Illustrated Presents Miami Heat*, June 25, 2006, p. 37.

6. Ibid. p. 39.

7. John Eligon, "Defending Heat Still Starts With O'Neal," *The New York Times*, May 24, 2006, p. C17.

8. Ibid.

9. Chris Mannix. "Taking The Giant, Final Step," *Sports Illustrated Presents Miami Heat*. June 25, 2006, p. 43.

10. Ibid. p. 59.

11. Tom Withers, "Miami 98, Dallas 96," *Yahoo Sports*, June 13, 2006, <http://sports.yahoo.com/nba/recap?gid=2006061314> (January 5, 2007).

12. Jack McCallum, "Down to the Wire," *Sports Illustrated*, June 26, 2006, p. 66.

13. Jack McCallum, "Flying Finish," *Sports Illustrated Presents Miami Heat*, June 25, 2006, p. 56.

14. Liz Robbins, "Pro Basketball; For Riley and Heat, a Long Chase Ends in Joy," *The New York Times*, June 22, 2006, <http://select.nytimes.com/gst/abstract.html?res=F10B14FD34550C718EDDAF0894DE404482> (December 1, 2006).

Chapter 2. 1988–1995

1. Bill Chastain, "The Heat is On: The Miami Heat's recipe for success," *Sport*, February 1993, p. 77.

2. Ron Rothstein, as quoted in "Sports People: Pro

Basketball; Rothstein Resigns as Coach of Heat," *nytimes .com,* May 2, 1991, <http://query.nytimes.com/gst/fullpage .html?res=9D0CE2DB1438F931A35756C0A967958> (January 5, 2007).

3. Jack McCallum, "Turn up the Heat, please," *Sports Illustrated.* December 19, 1988, p. 19.

4. Rick Braun, "Heat's New Owner Dumps Loughery," *Milwaukee Sentinel,* February 15, 1995, <http://www .findarticles.com/p/articles/mi_qn4208/is_19950215/ai_ n10185303> (January 5, 2007).

5. Ibid.

6. Glen Rice as told to Brett Ballantini, "Glen Rice—The Game I'll Never Forget," *NBA.com,* n.d., <http://www.nba .com/heat/history/gnf0506_rice.html> (January 5, 2007).

Chapter 3. 1995–2000

1. Kurt Rambis, as posted on "Rambo on Thunder," *NBA.com,* March 7, 2003, <http://www.nba.com/suns/ news/majerle_rambis.html> (January 5, 2007).

2. Glen Rice as told to Brett Ballantini, "Glen Rice—The Game I'll Never Forget," *NBA.com,* n.d., <http://www.nba .com/heat/history/gnf0506_rice.html> (January 5, 2007).

3. Ibid.

4. Jamal Mashburn, as posted as "Childs' Play: Guard Leads Knicks to Another Series Win Over Miami," *CNN Sports Illustrated,* May 22, 2000, <http://sportsillustrated .cnn.com/basketball/nba/2000/playoffs/news/2000/05/21 /knicks_heat_ap/> (January 5, 2007).

Chapter 4. 2000–2004

1. Tim Crothers, "Sweet Revenge: Coach Paul Silas and the Hornets settled old scores with lopsided new ones in a sweep of the favored Heat," *Sports Illustrated,* May 7, 2001, p. 40.

2. Ibid.

3. "Bringin' 'em off the beach," *St. Petersburg Times,* June 19, 2006, p. 5C.

4. Associated Press, "Stan Van Gundy Named New Heat Coach," *ESPN360,* October 25, 2003, <http://sports.espn .go.com/nba/news/story?id=1645777> (January 5, 2007).

5. Ibid.

6. Ibid.

Chapter 5. Front Office Firestarters

1. "Billy Cunningham Bio," *NBA Encyclopedia Playoff Edition,* 2007, <http://www.nba.com/history/players/cunningham_bio.html> (January 5, 2007).

2. Ibid.

3. Ibid.

4. Brian Mahoney, "Arison more than just 'other owner,'" *Sarasota Herald Tribune,* June 14, 2006, p. 6C.

Chapter 7. Miami Heat Stars

1. David DuPree, "It's Official: Shaq Traded to Heat for Three Players, Draft Pick," *USA Today,* July 15, 2004, <http://www.usatoday.com/sports/basketball/nba/2004-07-14-shaq-trade_x.htm> (January 5, 2007).

2. Ted Spiker, "Speed Profile: Dwyane Wade, Shooting Guard for the Miami Heat," *Men's Health,* 2006.

3. Andrea N. Whittaker, "The Great Defenders: The NBA's Top Stoppers Reveal How They Shut Down the Competition," *Sports Illustrated for Kids,* March 1, 2000. p. 42.

4. Glen Rice as told to Brett Ballantini, "Glen Rice—The Game I'll Never Forget," *NBA.com,* n.d., <http://www.nba.com/heat/history/gnf0506_rice.html> (January 5, 2007).

5. Bruce Newman, "To the point: guard Tim Hardaway, an unlikely Warrior No.1 draft choice, has become an NBA All-Star," *Sports Illustrated,* February 11, 1991, p. 52.

6. Roscoe Nance, "Heat's Eddie Jones happy to do whatever it takes," *USA Today,* May 11, 2005, <http://www.usatoday.com/sports/basketball/nba/heat/2005-05-11-eddie-jones_x.htm> (December 1, 2006).

Christopher, Matt. *On the Court with . . . Shaquille O'Neal.* New York: Little, Brown, and Company, 2003.

Gigliotti, Jim. *The Atlantic Division: the Boston Celtics, the Miami Heat, the New Jersey Nets, the New York Knicks, the Orlando Magic, the Philadelphia 76ers, and the Washington Wizards.* Chanhassen, Minn.: Child's World, 2004.

Gilbert, Sara. *The Story of the Miami Heat.* Mankato, Minn.: Creative Education, 2006.

Hareas, John. *NBA Slam.* New York: Scholastic, 2000.

Herzog, Brad. *Hoopmania: The Book of Basketball History and Trivia.* New York: Rosen Pub. Group, 2003.

Miller, Raymond H. *Shaquille O'Neal.* San Diego, Calif.: Kidhaven Press, 2003.

Nichols, John. *The History of the Miami Heat.* Mankato, Minn.: Creative Education, 2002.

Rosenthal, Bert. *Tim Hardaway: Star Guard.* Berkeley Heights, N.J.: Enslow Publishers, 2001.

Savage, Jeff. *Dwyane Wade.* Minneapolis, Minn.: Lerner Publications Co., 2007.

Stewart, Mark and Matt Zeysing. *The Miami Heat.* Chicago: Norwood House Press, 2006.

Stern, David J. *The Official NBA Basketball Encyclopedia.* New York: Doubleday, 2000.

Torres, John Albert. *Shaquille O'Neal: Gentle Giant.* Berkeley Heights, N.J.: Enslow Publishers, 2004.